RAND ARROYO CENTER

T0108938

War with China

Thinking Through the Unthinkable

David C. Gompert, Astrid Stuth Cevallos, Cristina L. Garafola

Prepared for the United States Army

Approved for public release; distribution unlimited

For more information on this publication, visit www.rand.org/t/rr1140

Library of Congress Cataloging-in-Publication Data is available
for this publication.

ISBN 978-0-8330-9155-0

Published by the RAND Corporation, Santa Monica, Calif.
© Copyright 2016 RAND Corporation
RAND® is a registered trademark.

Support RAND
Make a tax-deductible charitable contribution at
www.rand.org/giving/contribute

www.rand.org

Preface

War between the United States and China could be so ruinous for both countries, for East Asia, and for the world that it might seem unthinkable. Yet it is not: China and the United States are at loggerheads over several regional disputes that could lead to military confrontation or even violence between them. Both countries have large concentrations of military forces operating in close proximity. If an incident occurred or a crisis overheated, both have an incentive to strike enemy forces before being struck by them. And if hostilities erupted, both have ample forces, technology, industrial might, and personnel to fight across vast expanses of land, sea, air, space, and cyberspace. Thus, Sino-U.S. war, perhaps a large and costly one, is not just thinkable; it needs more thought.

In the United States—as, evidently, in China—systematic analysis of war has been the province of war planners. This is not good enough, for war planners are concerned mainly with how to gain military advantage, not how to avoid economic and political damage. Yet the consequences of war could go far beyond military success and failure: The world economy could be rocked, and international order, such as it is, could be shattered. Because the scope and effects of a Sino-U.S. war could be much wider than the scope of military planning for such a war, it is crucial to think and plan much more expansively than we have in the past.

At the same time, improvements in Chinese military capabilities mean that a war would not necessarily go the way U.S. war planners plan it. Whereas a clear U.S. victory once seemed probable, it is increasingly likely that a conflict could involve inconclusive fighting with steep losses on both sides. The United States cannot expect to control a conflict it cannot dominate militarily. While planning to win a war with China remains necessary, it is no longer sufficient: The United States must also consider how to limit war and its costs.

This study seeks to begin filling the hole in thinking about Sino-U.S. war by examining alternative paths one might take, effects on both countries of each path, preparations the United States should make, and ways to balance U.S. war aims against costs should war occur. It considers not only military factors but also economic, domestic political, and international ones, across the time frame from 2015 to 2025. Implications for the U.S. Army are highlighted. The authors emphasize that this analysis is indicative, not definitive, and that the findings are preliminary. It is hoped that this study will encourage others, for it is not meant to be the last word.

This research was sponsored by the Office of the Undersecretary of the Army and conducted within the RAND Arroyo Center's Strategy, Doctrine, and Resources Program. RAND Arroyo Center, part of the RAND Corporation, is a federally funded research and development center sponsored by the United States Army.

The Project Unique Identification Code (PUIC) for the project that produced this document is HQD146848.

Contents

Figures and Tables

Figures

Tables

Summary

As its military advantage declines, the United States will be less confident that a war with China will conform to its plans. China's improved military capabilities, particularly for anti-access and area denial (A2AD), mean that the United States cannot count on gaining operational control, destroying China's defenses, and achieving decisive victory if a war occurred. With that in mind, this report examines alternative paths that a war between the United States and China might take, losses and other effects on both sides, preparations that the United States should make, and ways to balance U.S. war aims against costs should war occur.

We postulate that a war would be regional and conventional. It would be waged mainly by ships on and beneath the sea, by aircraft and missiles of many sorts, and in space (against satellites) and cyberspace (against computer systems). We assume that fighting would start and remain in East Asia, where potential Sino-U.S. flash points and nearly all Chinese forces are located. Each side's increasingly far-flung disposition of forces and growing ability to track and attack opposing forces could turn much of the Western Pacific into a "war zone," with grave economic consequences. It is unlikely that nuclear weapons would be used: Even in an intensely violent conventional conflict, neither side would regard its losses as so serious, its prospects so dire, or the stakes so vital that it would run the risk of devastating nuclear retaliation by using nuclear weapons first. We also assume that China would not attack the U.S. homeland, except via cyberspace, given its minimal capability to do so with conventional weapons. In contrast,

U.S. nonnuclear attacks against military targets in China could be extensive. The time frame studied is 2015 to 2025.

The need to think through war with China is made all the more important by developments in military capabilities. Sensors, weapon guidance, digital networking, and other information technologies used to target opposing forces have advanced to the point where *both* U.S. and Chinese military forces seriously threaten *each other*. This creates the means as well as the incentive to strike enemy forces before they strike one's own. In turn, this creates a bias toward sharp, reciprocal strikes from the outset of a war, yet with neither side able to gain control and both having ample capacity to keep fighting, even as military losses and economic costs mount.

A Sino-U.S. conflict is unlikely to involve large land combat. Moreover, the unprecedented ability of U.S. and Chinese forces to target and destroy each other—*conventional counterforce*—could greatly deplete military capabilities in a matter of months. After that, the sides could replenish and improve their forces in an industrial-technological-demographic mobilization contest, the outcome of which depends on too many factors to speculate, except to say that costs would continue to climb.

While the primary audience for this study is the U.S. policy community, we hope that Chinese policymakers will also think through possible courses and consequences of war with the United States, including potential damage to China's economic development and threats to China's equilibrium and cohesion. We find little in the public domain to indicate that the Chinese political leadership has given this matter the attention it deserves.

Four Analytic Cases

The path of war might be defined mainly by two variables: intensity (from mild to severe) and duration (from a few days to a year or more). Thus, we analyze four cases: brief and severe, long and severe, brief and mild, and long and mild. The main determinant of intensity is whether, at the outset, U.S. and Chinese political leaders grant or deny their respective militaries permission to execute their plans to attack opposing forces unhesitatingly. The main determinant of duration, given that both powers have the material wherewithal to fight a long war, is whether and when at least one side loses the will to fight or calculates that continuing to do so would be counterproductive.

We categorize the effects of each case as military, economic, domestic political, and international. Military losses include aircraft, surface ships, submarines, missile launchers and inventories, and C4ISR (command, control, communications, computing, intelligence, surveillance, and reconnaissance) systems, which are increasingly vulnerable to cyber and anti-satellite (ASAT) warfare. Economic costs include the contraction of trade, consumption, and revenue from investments abroad. (The disruption of energy supplies is captured in the effects of trade contraction.) Should cyberwarfare escalate from military to civilian domains and infect critical information infrastructure, economic activity could be further disrupted. Domestic political effects could range from impeding war policy to endangering internal stability. International responses could be supportive, opposed, or destabilizing.

The current rate of advances in military technology, especially in Chinese A2AD and in cyberwar and ASAT capabilities of both sides, implies a potential for major change in the decade to come, which dictates examining 2025 cases distinct from 2015 cases. Economic conditions will also change between now and 2025—with the Chinese economy potentially overtaking the U.S. economy, Chinese investments abroad growing, and both economies relying more than ever on computer networking—though not enough to alter qualitatively the economic impact of a war. Attempting to specify domestic political and international effects of war a decade from now would be even more speculative. Thus, 2025 is analyzed distinctly from 2015 only in the military dimension.

The four cases and indicative findings about losses, costs, and other effects are as follows:

- *Brief, severe:* If either U.S. or Chinese political leaders authorize their military commanders to carry out plans for sharp strikes on enemy forces, a severely violent war would erupt. As of 2015, U.S. losses of surface naval and air forces, including disabled aircraft carriers and regional air bases, could be significant, but Chinese losses, including to homeland-based A2AD systems, would be much greater. Within days, it would be apparent to both sides that the early gap in losses favoring the United States would widen if fighting continued. By 2025, though, U.S. losses would increase because of enhanced Chinese A2AD. This, in turn, could limit Chinese losses, though these would still be greater than U.S. ones. It could be unclear then whether continued fighting would result in victory for either side. Economically, even a brief, severe war would produce a shock to Chinese global trade, most of which would have to transit the Western Pacific war zone, whereas U.S. economic damage would largely be confined to bilateral trade with China. International and domestic political responses would have little impact.

- *Long, severe:* As of 2015, the longer a severe war dragged on, the worse the results and prospects would be for China. By 2025, however, inconclusive results in early fighting could motivate both sides to fight on despite heavy losses incurred and still expected. Although prospects for U.S. military victory then would be worse than they are today, this would not necessarily imply Chinese victory. As the fighting persisted, much of the Western Pacific, from the Yellow Sea to the South China Sea, could become hazardous for commercial sea and air transport. Sharply reduced trade, including energy supplies, could harm China's economy disproportionately and badly. The longer and harsher a conflict, the greater would be the likelihood of involving other states, especially U.S. allies in the region—most importantly, Japan.

- *Brief, mild:* Given the uncertain prospects of swift military victory, the risks of losing control, and the specter of major economic damage, both Chinese and U.S. leaders—for it would take *both*—might decline to authorize all-out strikes on the other side's forces. What could follow is tightly restricted, low-grade, sporadic, inconclusive fighting, with minimal military losses. Assuming that leaders of both states were inclined and had enough political latitude to compromise, such a conflict could be ended before it produced major economic damage or domestic and international political tremors.

- *Long, mild:* With fighting contained and losses tolerable, the sides could try to escape the political costs of compromise by continuing a low-grade conflict. Because neither would gain the upper hand militarily, this could go on for some time. In the meantime, even with fighting limited, economic losses would grow, especially for China. With the passage of time, domestic and international political reactions would intensify, though less consequentially than in the long, severe case.

These cases indicate that the advanced conventional counterforce capabilities of both the United States and China could produce major military losses from the outset and throughout unrestrained (though nonnuclear) hostilities. Once *either* military is authorized to commence strikes, the ability of *both* to control the conflict would be greatly compromised. Each side could regard preemptive attack on the other's forces as a way to gain a major early and sustainable edge in losses and thus in capabilities to prevail; this underscores the instability inherent in mutual, conventional counterforce capabilities and warfighting concepts.

By 2025, enhanced Chinese A2AD will have shrunk the gap between Chinese and U.S. military losses: Chinese losses would still be very heavy; U.S. losses, though less than China's, could be much heavier than in a 2015 war. Even as U.S. military victory became less likely, Chinese victory would remain elusive. Because both sides would be able to continue to inflict severe losses, neither one would likely be willing to accept defeat. History offers no encouragement that destructive but stalemated fighting induces belligerents to agree to stop. A severe, lengthy, militarily inconclusive war would weaken and leave both powers vulnerable to other threats.

The Importance of Nonmilitary Factors

The prospect of a military standoff means that war could eventually be decided by nonmilitary factors. These should favor the United States now and in the future. Although war would harm both economies, damage to China's could be catastrophic and lasting: on the order of a 25–35 percent reduction in Chinese gross domestic product (GDP) in a yearlong war, compared with a reduction in U.S. GDP on the order of 5–10 percent. Even a mild conflict, unless ended promptly, could weaken China's economy. A long and severe war could ravage China's economy, stall its hard-earned development, and cause widespread hardship and dislocation.

Such economic damage could in turn aggravate political turmoil and embolden separatists in China. Although the regime and its security forces presumably could withstand such challenges, doing so might necessitate increased oppressiveness, tax the capacity, and undermine the legitimacy of the Chinese regime in the midst of a very difficult war. In contrast, U.S. domestic partisan skirmishing could handicap the war effort but not endanger societal stability, much less the survival of the state, no matter how long and harsh the conflict, so long as it remains conventional. Escalating cyberwarfare, while injurious to both sides, could worsen China's economic problems and impede the government's ability to control a restive population.

International responses could, on balance, also favor the United States in a long and severe war: The support of U.S. East Asian allies could hurt China's military chances; responses of Russia, India, and NATO would have less impact; and NATO could neutralize Russian opportunistic threats in Europe. Japan's entry would be likely if the nation were party to the underlying dispute and almost certain if its territory (where U.S. bases are) were attacked. With Tokyo's more permissive interpretation of constitutional limits on use of force and programmed improvements in Japanese military capabilities, Japan's entry could make a difference by 2025 in the course and results of war. Heightened turmoil in the Middle East could be harmful to both Chinese and U.S. interests.

These findings reinforce the widely held view that a Sino-U.S. war would be so harmful that both states should place a very high priority on avoiding one. While expectations of huge costs make premeditated war improbable, they also demand strong crisis management and civilian control of the military by both governments. Given the extreme penalty for allowing one's forces to be struck before they strike, creating mutual forbearance at the outset of hostilities could be as difficult as it is critical. It requires an ability to cooperate, in effect, even after fighting has begun. Thus, the need for instant and unfiltered leader-to-leader communication is as great when hostilities begin as it is during crises that could lead to them.

Because the United States might be unable to control, win, or avoid major losses and costs from a severe conflict, it must guard against automaticity in executing, if not initiating, a sharp and prompt counterforce exchange. This demands fail-safe assurance of definitive presidential approval to carry out military plans, which in turn requires that military commanders provide the president with a range of feasible options.

Notwithstanding its improved A2AD capabilities, China has even more to lose from a severe conflict, yet it has less experience with civilian-military coordination during high-tech, high-speed warfare. China's leaders would be ill-advised to think that trends in military modernization point to a brief and successful war. More likely is a severe, drawn-out, militarily inconclusive one, with economic, political, and international effects that might favor the United States. China has as much cause as the United States to prevent automatic execution of military plans for a prompt and sharp counterforce exchange, including an unambiguous requirement for political decisionmaking.

Recommended Actions for the U.S. Military

Chinese restraint in attacking U.S. forces when hostilities begin depends on Chinese expectations of U.S. action. The U.S. military should not rely on plans to destroy China's A2AD capabilities in the first moments of a conflict. Such reliance could undermine crisis stability, predispose the Chinese toward preemptive strikes, and heighten the danger of automaticity and inevitability of fierce fighting from the outset. Furthermore, the U.S. military should not prejudge or limit the president's options by having only a plan for immediate conventional counterforce attack, nor leave itself unprepared to carry out alternative plans. It would be far better for stability and at least as good for deterrence for the U.S. military to emphasize, in general, planning for a prolonged high-intensity war and to make this emphasis known to China. Signaling a specific predisposition to strike Chinese A2AD capabilities before they could be used against U.S. forces increases the risk that those capabilities would be used before they were themselves struck.

In parallel with measures to prevent crises from becoming violent and violence from becoming severe, the United States should try to reduce the impact of Chinese A2AD by investing in more-survivable weapons platforms and in its own A2AD capabilities: missiles, submarines, drones and drone-launching platforms, cyber, and ASAT. Such capabilities would deny the Chinese confidence of victory and would improve stability in crises, as well as in the critical initial stage of a conflict. But they would not restore U.S. military dominance and control or spare the United States major losses or economic costs in a severe conflict.

While keeping in mind the potentially huge costs of preparing comprehensively for a low-probability war with China, the United States should make certain prudent preparations:

- improve the ability to sustain and survive severely intense military operations
- enhance high-priority military capabilities of, and military interoperability with, allies and partners near China
- conduct contingency planning with Japan and other East Asian allies and partners
- consult with NATO regarding contingencies involving conflict with China, including possible Russian and Iranian reactions
- adopt measures to mitigate the interruption of critical products from China

- formulate options to deny China access to war-critical imports (e.g., fuels).

The U.S. Army, in its Title X and joint responsibilities, can contribute by

- investing in counter-A2AD capabilities—for example, mobile land-based missiles and integrated air defense to worsen expected Chinese military, naval, and air losses
- strengthening, advising, and enabling East Asian partners to mount strong defense
- assessing high-demand weapons and stocks in the event of a long, severe war.

Because such U.S. measures could be interpreted as hostile by the Chinese, the United States, including the U.S. Army, should also expand and deepen Sino-U.S. military-to-military understanding and measures to reduce risks of misperception and miscalculation.

Conclusion

Although advances in targeting enable conventional counterforce warfare and reduce U.S. warfighting dominance, they do not point to Chinese dominance or victory. War between the two countries could begin with devastating strikes; be hard to control; last months, if not years; have no winner; and inflict huge losses on both sides' military forces. The longer such a war would rage, the greater the importance of economic, domestic political, and international effects. While such nonmilitary effects would fall hardest on China, they could also greatly harm the U.S. economy and the United States' ability to meet challenges worldwide. The United States should make sensible preparations to wage a long and fierce war with China. But it should also develop plans to limit the scope, intensity, and duration of a war; tighten up its system of civilian control; and expand communications with China in times of peace, crisis, and war.

Acknowledgments

The authors are most fortunate to have had the steady hand and thoughtful advice of RAND colleague Terrence Kelly in helping conceive, design, and conduct this study. They thank him and the rest of the Arroyo Center team for their strong support. The authors also want to recognize colleagues Howard Shatz and Duncan Long for providing invaluable ideas on method and substance. Toward the end of our work, Jerry Sollinger came in from the bullpen to make this report as readable as we hope it is. Good reports typically mean that they have gone through painstaking quality review. We thank Larry Cavaiola, Keith Crane, and Tim Heath for pressing us hard but constructively to improve our work. Finally, our editor, Rebecca Fowler, deserves the authors' gratitude for getting our prose up to the standards RAND readers expect. Despite all this help, any mistakes are exclusively the authors' responsibility.

CHAPTER ONE

Introduction

The ambitious should consider above all that [with] an equality of force between belligerent parties, all that princes can expect from the greatest advantages at present is to acquire . . . some territory which will not pay the interest on the expenses of war, and whose population does not even approach the number of citizens who perished in the campaign.[1]

—Frederick the Great

Purpose

For all the studies and opinion pieces about how a war with China might start and should be fought, one finds little serious analysis, at least in the public domain, of what such a war might be like and what its consequences could be. This is a gaping omission, for China is at loggerheads with the United States over several regional disputes that could lead to military confrontation or even violence, and both superpowers have ample forces, industrial might, and people to fight long and hard across a vast expanse of land, sea, air, space, and cyberspace. This study seeks to start filling this gap by examining the alternative paths that a war between the United States and China might take, effects of each path on both sides, preparations the United States should make, and ways to balance U.S. war aims against costs should

---

[1] Frederick the Great quoted by Geoffrey Parker, "The Military Revolution," in Lawrence Freedman, ed., *War*, Oxford, UK: Oxford University Press, Oxford, 1994, p. 247.

war occur.[2] The study considers not only military factors but also economic, domestic political, and international ones, across a time frame from 2015 to 2025. Implications for the U.S. Army are highlighted.

While our primary audience consists of American policymakers and planners, we hope that their Chinese counterparts will also think through possible paths and consequences of war, for it could destroy much of what modern China has accomplished. There is no indication that the Chinese have given the potential impact of a war the rigorous attention it warrants.

Rationale

The need to think through war with China is made all the more pressing by developments in military technology and associated doctrine: Sensors, global positioning, weapon guidance, digital networking, and other capabilities used to target opposing forces have advanced to the point where *both* U.S. and Chinese military forces pose serious threats to each other. This creates the ability and a reason to strike enemy forces before they strike one's own, which is bound to influence both nations' war planning.[3] Military technology and planning are thus creating a bias toward sharp exchange of strikes from the start, with both

---

[2] Perhaps the two most definitive U.S. official annual documents are the U.S. Department of Defense annual report to Congress, *Military and Security Developments Involving the People's Republic of China*, and the annual report of the joint Congressional-Executive Commission on China. Neither contains analysis of the range of possibilities and consequences of war with China. See Office of the Secretary of Defense, *Annual Report to Congress: Military and Security Developments Involving the People's Republic of China 2014*, Washington, D.C., April 24, 2014; and Congressional-Executive Commission on China, *2014 Annual Report*, Washington, D.C., October 9, 2014.

[3] Chinese warfighting doctrine is laid out in the People's Liberation Army's (PLA's) *Science of Military Strategy* and *Science of Campaigns*. (See Peng Guangqian and Yao Youzhi, eds., *Science of Military Strategy* [*Zhanlue Xue*], Beijing: Military Science Press, 2005; and Zhang Yuliang, ed., *Science of Campaigns* [*Zhanyi Xue*], Beijing: National Defense University Press, 2006.) The implication of U.S. reliance on attacking China's A2AD is found in various public explanations of the U.S. Navy and U.S. Air Force Air-Sea Battle concept, which has been subsumed under the Joint Concept for Access and Maneuver (see, for example, U.S. Naval Institute, "Document: Air Sea Battle Name Change Memo," January 20, 2015).

sides intent on gaining the upper hand or at least denying it to the other. To quote Chinese strategists: "[I]t has become possible to achieve operational objectives before an enemy can make a response. . . . If the PLA [People's Liberation Army] fights with a high-tech and powerful enemy, we must achieve operational suddenness."[4] The combination of such confidence and urgency might be misplaced and dangerous—and not just for China.

A hazard inherent in all war planning is that it sets and limits expectations of what will actually occur. Only a militarily dominant belligerent can afford to be so cavalier, and when it comes to China, the United States is no longer dominant, nor can it afford to be cavalier. As its military advantages vis-à-vis China decline, the United States can be less confident that war would conform to its plans. Improved Chinese forces, particularly for anti-access and area denial (A2AD), means that the United States cannot be sanguine about gaining operational control, destroying China's defenses, and achieving decisive victory if a war occurred.

Because Sino-U.S. war could be extremely costly even for the victor, it is not likely to result from premeditated attack by either side. Yet Sino-U.S. crises could occur and involve incidents or miscalculations that lead to hostilities. China could try to intimidate its neighbors below the threshold of U.S. intervention, yet misjudge where that threshold is. China could underestimate U.S. willingness to back Japan militarily in a crisis over disputed territory in the East China Sea. Moreover, the contradiction between China's claim of sovereignty over its 200-nautical-mile Exclusive Economic Zone (EEZ) and U.S. insistence that such zones are international waters beyond 12 nautical miles could bring forces into close and hazardous proximity if either side opts to enforce its stance.

A case in point of how conflicting Chinese and U.S. views could lead to war is found in the South China Sea. In support of China's

---

[4] Zhang, 2006, p. 96. See also Jianxiang Bi, "Joint Operations: Developing a New Paradigm," in James Mulvenon and David M. Finkelstein, eds., *China's Revolution in Doctrinal Affairs: Emerging Trends in the Operational Art of the Chinese People's Liberation Army,* Washington, D.C.: CNA Corporation, December 2005, especially pp. 47–49.

objective of making virtually the entire South China Sea sovereign territorial waters, China has been building artificial islands, airstrips, and other militarily useful infrastructure—and claiming 200-mile EEZs around them. The United States will not accept this because it runs afoul of several U.S. interests: the principle of peaceful settlement of disputes, the principle of freedom of the seas, the fact that some 40 percent of world trade passes through the South China Sea, and the expectations of the Philippines and other U.S. friends that the United States will not condone Chinese unilateral action. Consequently, the Americans have steamed naval surface combatants through the very waters China is claiming and on which it is building. There seems little doubt that the Chinese will operate forces in these contested waters, in which case Chinese and U.S. forces will be present and actively shadowing or constricting the other side's forces. If, or as, a crisis occurs, the risk of a spark causing inadvertent conflict would be heightened, perhaps greatly. Moreover, political leaders on both sides may become less flexible, not more, with so much at stake, and military commanders could urge in favor of escalation either to deter or to prepare for conflict. While current odds strongly favor the United States militarily in the South China Sea, making Beijing more likely than Washington to back down, the improvement and extension of Chinese A2AD in that direction could make a crisis harder to defuse. As horrific as a Sino-U.S. war could be, it cannot be considered implausible.

As we will see, the cause of war and the importance each side attaches to it could affect how fiercely and long it will fight, though hostilities can create dynamics and fury that eclipse rational calculation. If both sides have substantial war-making capacity and neither one can gain operational dominance and control, there is a danger of prolonged ferocious fighting at great cost, even though both might plan and expect it to end quickly. Such conditions recall those of Europe in 1914, when a crisis triggered near-automatic execution of military plans to attack before being attacked, when the economies of the two sides were interlocked, and when both foresaw a short war. As fighting raged, casualties soared, and territory was lost and won, the belligerents found themselves fighting over far more than an incident involving Serbian nationalists seeking to end Austria-Hungary's control of Bosnia-Herzegovina. Now, as then, the result could be huge military losses (then in foot soldiers, now in weapon platforms) and lasting economic damage on both sides.

In sum, the risk that some Sino-U.S. confrontation will lead to hostilities, the declining ability of the United States to gain military-operational control, the conventional counterforce capabilities (the capabilities of U.S. and Chinese forces to target and destroy each other) of both militaries, the vulnerability of both economies, and the potential for prolonged fighting with devastating results demand fresh but sober thinking about Sino-U.S. war. Because war with China, seen in this light, is not implausible and could be very dangerous and very demanding, the United States must be prepared for it. Already, military requirements for a Sino-U.S. war figure prominently in U.S. force planning and operating concepts (as they do in China's). But larger national requirements, depending on the war's intensity and duration, have not received equivalent attention. Both the United States and China need to be aware of what the costs of war might be. If advances in conventional counterforce capabilities are making war harder to control, leaders need political instruments to keep combat from destroying more than it can gain.

Factors Considered

As U.S. military dominance wanes, U.S. strategists must consider (as this study does) a range of contingencies and corresponding requirements. Recent research on strategic decisionmaking finds that unjustified faith in the ability to plan, control, and limit the duration of fighting is a common mistake in starting wars that end badly. After analyzing numerous historical cases, a RAND study concluded that "confidence that an adversary will comply with one's script and . . . that the results of a decision can be controlled is tantamount to assuming away risk. When this leads to failure to prepare for bad results, the consequences can be that much worse."[5]

Essential though it is for U.S. armed forces to have plans to fight and win, excessive confidence in such plans could have detrimental effects on U.S. peacetime policy, crisis management, and wartime operations. At worst, inattention to the range of possible paths and consequences of war with China could lead the United States into one for which it is unprepared. Likewise, the Chinese would be profoundly wrong to think that improving their military capabilities would make a war with the United States controllable, winnable, and affordable.[6] As we will see, it could be that neither country is able to control, win, or afford a future war.

Paradoxically, as both sides hone their military strategies with the aim of controlling a war, they reduce the possibility of control. Military officers of both countries have spoken and written about how to achieve operational advantage, or at least avoid disadvantage, by striking the other side's forces at the outset of a conflict.[7] Given the "first-mover" advantage and the corresponding danger that perception of a climbing probability of hostilities would increase the pressure on each side's trigger finger, the goal of avoiding a war must compete with that of winning one. Likewise, as we will see, the goal of winning a war must be weighed against the goal of containing its costs. Given the potential military, economic, and political costs of a long conflict, each side wants to succeed quickly. Accordingly, the Chinese stress the need to strike intervening U.S. forces early and then to limit the duration and scope of fighting that ensues, especially by preventing attacks

---

[5]   David C. Gompert, Hans Binnendijk, and Bonny Lin, *Blinders, Blunders, and Wars: What America and China Can Learn*, Santa Monica, Calif.: RAND Corporation, RR-768-RC, 2014.

[6]   The Chinese appear to be aware of how costly war with the United States could be (see David Finkelstein, "Chinese Perceptions of the Costs of a Conflict," in Andrew Scobell, ed., *The Costs of Conflict: The Impact on China of a Future War*, Carlisle, Pa.: Strategic Studies Institute, 2001, pp. 9–28).

[7]   See David C. Gompert and Terrence K. Kelly, "Escalation Cause: How the Pentagon's New Strategy Could Trigger War with China," *Foreign Policy*, August 3, 2013, among others articles on Air-Sea Battle.

on China itself. In turn, U.S. warfighting concepts rest on the logic that gaining operational control, limiting losses, and achieving victory might depend on disabling Chinese A2AD capabilities before they can be used to full effect to disable U.S. forces.

The strong preference of both states to avoid a long war is only natural, given expected military losses and other costs. Yet the very military strategies that call for each to strike the other's forces hard and early, perhaps preemptively, could work against a war-ending compromise and lead to the prolongation and expansion of war. Consider the major wars of the 20th century, in which the side that attacked first— Germany twice and Japan once—summoned the other side's will to fight, persevere, and ultimately prevail.[8] Indeed, it is wise to heed the simple verity that striking first does not ensure victory. Moreover, the path of a Sino-U.S. war might be determined not just by military operations but also by economic, political, and international effects and pressures. We will see that the longer war lasts, the more important nonmilitary factors might become.

The assumption that a Sino-U.S. war would be over quickly is not supported by evidence that either side would rapidly exhaust its warmaking capacity. China and the United States have considerable military, economic, industrial, and demographic depth. If China is vulnerable to critical shortages in a war with the United States, it could be in losses of frontline military systems—its backup forces being largely obsolescent—or in oil supplies, of which it imports about 60 percent and has a declared strategic reserve of just ten days or so.[9]

As important as physical wherewithal is the political stamina of the two states. At first, the Chinese government could largely ignore domestic opposition, whereas the U.S. government could not. Yet the legitimacy of the Chinese state rests on its ability to provide for the material needs and improve the living standards of the population, which would be at risk by a costly war. Just as political will could deter-

---

[8] Germany's initial offensives on both fronts in both world wars and Japan's attack on Pearl Harbor appeared successful, but ultimately both countries were defeated.

[9] "China Makes First Announcement on Strategic Oil Reserves," Reuters, November 20, 2014.

mine a war's duration, the war's dynamics—military success or failure, casualties, costs, and expectations of what further fighting might bring—could determine will. All else being equal, the more even the military capabilities, the less likely that one side's will would crack before the other's.

Finally, willingness to suffer losses and support prolonged fighting could be affected by the perceived stakes of the conflict. Thus, the path *to* war could affect the path *of* war, including its severity and duration. Consider several situations that could turn violent:

- Sino-Japanese skirmishing over disputed territory in the East China Sea, where the United States has said its defense treaty with Japan applies
- Chinese harassment to press its territorial claims in (and to) the South China Sea—against the Philippines or Vietnam, for example—in the face of U.S. insistence on peaceful dispute resolution and freedom of the seas
- uncoordinated military interventions by Chinese, South Korean, or U.S. forces in the event of a collapse of North Korea
- Chinese threat or use of force to intimidate or seize Taiwan
- an incident at sea, such as the downing of an aircraft, owing to forces operating in close proximity, perhaps in EEZ waters claimed as sovereign by China but as commons by the United States.

To illustrate, the United States might be willing to fight resolutely to prevent China from gaining control of the South China Sea, whereas China might seek a peaceful solution in the face of such American resolve. In contrast, the Chinese might be more determined to prevent Taiwan's independence from China than the United States is to prevent Taiwan's forcible unification with China. The analysis that follows does not deal with the merits of Sino-American quarrels or the probability that they will lead to war, but it does recognize that asymmetric interests can result in asymmetric resolve in the face of losses.

These factors suggest a need to examine with rigor how a Sino-U.S. war might be fought, how long it might last, and how its mounting costs and shifting outlook could affect the ability and will of each side to keep fighting. One hundred years ago, European leaders and strategists, having formed alliances and adopted mobilization plans that would lead readily, if not automatically, from confrontation to war, erred further by assuming that war would be brief, either because their side would win quickly or because both sides would want to end the war before their armies and interlocking economies were devastated. Yet for four years neither side would compromise to end the stalemated carnage. A Sino-U.S. war would hold similar dangers: an incentive to strike first and a belief that fighting would end quickly and limit costs. Such thinking could turn a crisis into a conflict and leave the United States unprepared if war occurred and turned out to be lengthy.

How This Report Is Organized

This study is preliminary and conceptual; its cases are imagined, and its estimates only illustrative. With these qualifications in mind, the chapters to come pursue the following line of inquiry:

- What are the parameters of a Sino-U.S. war?
- How do Chinese and U.S. planners think about how such a war should or would proceed?
- What variables would describe a Sino-U.S. war?
- What different paths do these variables suggest?
- What military consequences and demands are implied by each path?
- What could be the impact on the U.S. and Chinese economies, on Sino-U.S. economic relations, on East Asian economies, and on the world economy?
- What internal political pressures and constraints could arise during a war?
- What international reactions might be expected?
- What are the implications for U.S. policy, requirements, and preparations, including expectations of the U.S. Army?

The report also has two appendixes, which provide additional information about possible military losses and economic effects.

CHAPTER TWO

Analytic Framework

We postulate that a war between the United States and China would be regional, conventional, and high-tech, and it would be waged mainly on and beneath the sea, in the air (with aircraft, drones, and missiles), in space, and in cyberspace. Although ground combat could occur in certain scenarios (e.g., a conflict over Korean unification), we exclude the possibility of a huge land war in Asia. We assume that fighting would start and remain in East Asia, where potential flash points and nearly all Chinese forces are located. Each side's increasingly far-flung regional disposition of forces and growing ability to track and attack opposing forces could turn much of the Western Pacific into a "war zone," with grave economic consequences. It is unlikely that nuclear weapons would be used: Even in an intensely violent conventional conflict, neither side would regard its losses as so serious, its prospects so dire, or the stakes so vital that it would run the risk of nuclear retaliation by using nuclear weapons first. We also assume that China would not attack the U.S. homeland, except via cyberspace, given China's minimal capability to do so with conventional weapons. In contrast, U.S. nonnuclear attacks against military targets in China could be extensive.

Two variables would largely define the path a war might take: intensity (from mild to severe) and duration (from a few days to a year or more); thus, we present four cases. The main determinant of intensity is whether, at the outset, U.S. and Chinese political leaders grant or deny their respective militaries permission to execute their plans to attack opposing forces unhesitatingly, which would precipitate severely intense combat. The main determinant of length, given that both powers have the potential to fight a long war, is whether and when either one loses the will to fight or concludes that continuing to do so would be counterproductive.

We categorize the effects of each case as military, economic, domestic political, and international. Military losses—that is, decline in military capabilities—would mainly consist of destroyed or disabled weapon platforms and systems and C4ISR (command, control, communications, computing, intelligence, surveillance, and reconnaissance). No attempt is made to analyze potential casualties, though very crude estimates could be derived from platform losses.[1] Economic costs are defined here as reductions in gross domestic product (GDP) from loss of trade, consumption, and income from investments abroad. The disruption of energy supplies is captured in effects of trade contraction. Costs of assets seized, forces destroyed, and infrastructure damaged, though potentially sizable, are excluded because they would not immediately affect GDP. Domestic political responses could involve support, impatience, opposition, instability, or impairment of the war effort. International responses could favor one side or the other, perhaps to the point of intervention, and could pressure one or both sides to cease fighting.

Our time frame is 2015–2025. The current rate of advances in military technology, especially in Chinese A2AD and in cyberwar and anti-satellite (ASAT) capabilities of both sides, implies a potential for major change in the decade to come, which dictates examining cases in 2025 distinct from cases in 2015. Economic conditions will also change between now and 2025—with China's economy possibly overtaking the U.S. economy in size, Chinese investments abroad growing, and both economies relying more than ever on computer networking—though not enough to alter qualitatively the economic impact of a war. Attempting to specify domestic political and international effects of

---

[1] Broadly stated, on the assumptions of no large land combat, extensive strategic bombing, or use of nuclear weapons, loss of life would be comparatively low and not a good index of the scale of fighting or costs.

war a decade from now would be even more speculative. Thus, 2025 is analyzed distinctly from 2015 only in the military dimension.

U.S. and Chinese Thinking About War

U.S. and Chinese thinking about war suggests that both sides expect a conflict to be sharp, with China planning (and hoping) for a short one, and the United States more confident of victory if fighting persists. As far as the public record shows, neither side has analyzed systematically the effects of a long war or seized on the idea (discussed later) of deliberately and mutually restricting the violence.

Chinese military thought has evolved since the early Maoist notions of "people's war" and a "war of annihilation" between diametrically opposed ideological systems. Emerging concepts reflect China's growing ability and inclination to threaten or use force for limited purposes nearby (e.g., blocking Taiwan's independence or enforcing maritime claims) without finding itself at war with the United States. Yet war with the United States cannot be excluded and could involve strikes on China, staggering losses and costs, and eventual defeat. So China has had to prepare, if it is unable to deter U.S. intervention, to avert defeat.[2]

This situation has stoked Chinese interest in A2AD—in essence, conventional counterforce—enabled especially by increasing Chinese prowess in targeting technologies.[3] A2AD raises the costs and thus the threshold of U.S. intervention in a conflict involving China. By reducing the U.S. threat to China, A2AD might build a shield behind which China might feel freer to use force. In addition, U.S. military advantages have steered Chinese thinking about warfighting toward taking the initiative, making sudden gains, degrading U.S. strike forces, and then limiting the ensuing conflict's geographic scope, weapons, targets, and duration. While the Chinese regard U.S. aircraft carriers and

---

[2] See, for example, Finkelstein, 2001, pp. 9–28.

[3] Chinese A2AD might also be motivated geopolitically by the desire to increase the vulnerability and thus reduce the presence of U.S. military strength in the Western Pacific.

regional air bases as prime targets, they also see C4ISR as an American Achilles' heel, and so have expanded their arsenal and planning to include cyberwar and ASAT.

However, China's risk in attempting to achieve a fait accompli is that the United States would strike back (or strike first), expand and extend the conflict, bring its warfighting superiority to bear, visit destruction on China itself, sever Chinese sea links, and impose a harsh peace. The Chinese ought also to worry, if they do not already, that a long war could cause internal instability and encourage separatism. In sum, the Chinese have scripted early strikes on U.S. forces and a quick cessation of hostilities, with little room for error.

In parallel with such Chinese thinking about how to fight, contain, and conclude a war with the United States, Chinese military strategists have taken interest in the idea of "war control."[4] This concept seeks to resolve the problem of how to avoid crushing defeat without giving up the option of using force when it is in China's interest to do so. Chinese thinking on war control goes like this: Overriding goals of national stability and development apply no less in war than in peace, dictating that China be able to control and limit war should it occur. Military initiative should be used to frame the scale, scope, and course of war, as well as to induce the enemy to end it on China's terms. It is essential not only to prevent expansion, escalation, and prolongation but also to guide combat toward an advantageous resolution at the lowest price to China. Therefore, forces and operations need to be controlled by political leaders who are mindful of China's transcendent goals. Throughout hostilities, China needs to assess progress and seize chances to end the war with a stable outcome that protects Chinese sovereignty, independence, territorial integrity, institutional security, and economic lifelines.[5]

---

4   See Lonnie Henley, "War Control: Chinese Concepts of Escalation Management," in Andrew Scobell and Larry M. Wortzel, eds., *Shaping China's Security Environment: The Role of the People's Liberation Army*, Carlisle, Pa.: Strategic Studies Institute, U.S. Army War College, 2006.

5   Liu Shenyang, "On War of Control—Mainly from the Military Thinking Perspective," *China Military Science*, April 2014. Liu is the deputy commander of the Jinan Military District and a lieutenant general of the PLA.

This is a tall order indeed, especially in a conflict with a stronger power. The Chinese are aware of this challenge, and they frequently discuss their prior success in defeating superior military powers despite inferior capabilities.[6] While Chinese emphasis on war control is not new, the Chinese might have growing confidence in its feasibility, owing to enhancement of Chinese A2AD and evidence that the United States is not invincible and is not guaranteed to retain control of a conflict: "No matter how strong a country may be, how mighty its military strength is, it is impossible [for it] to take total control of the entire situation. The United States launched wars in Afghanistan and Iraq [and] is still trapped."[7]

Increasing belief in China's ability to manage crises and war proactively, rather than reacting or having to launch an all-or-nothing opening salvo, could embolden Chinese behavior in peace and crises. It could also affect the path that a Sino-U.S. war could take. While consistent with the concept of early attacks on U.S. strike forces, war control contemplates "conflict in its entirety," including *postwar* China, Asia, and the world. It suggests the Chinese are mindful of the need to balance war aims against costs should war occur. More specifically, postulating that controlling the scale, scope, and duration of hostilities could be critical implies Chinese awareness of possibilities other than fierce conventional counterforce exchanges. One such possibility is that Chinese civilian leaders would try to keep hostilities limited, hoping that U.S. war-weariness delivers a settlement favoring China. In any case, President Xi Jinping's efforts to strengthen political control over the PLA speak to a critical prerequisite of war control.

U.S. thinking about war is also in flux. For some time, the United States was confident that its vastly superior strike power could destroy Chinese forces straightaway. Of course, even with Chinese naval and air forces shattered, the United States knows it would struggle mightily and pay dearly if it engaged in land war on Chinese soil (an idea then–U.S. Defense Secretary Robert Gates famously suggested would war-

---

[6] See Zhang, 2006.

[7] Liu, 2014.

rant psychiatric treatment for U.S. leaders[8]). As China's A2AD capabilities improve, the United States has begun to consider striking them before losing its strike forces.[9] While there is operational logic to this, the fact that Chinese A2AD systems are mainly homeland-based raises risks of escalation, as well as risks of crisis instability insofar as it could prompt the Chinese to strike preemptively.

In addition to reflecting Chinese and U.S. doctrine, the intensity and duration of a war could depend on the command and control (C2) precepts and practices of the two sides. U.S. C2 increasingly stresses flexibility, subordinate initiative, responsiveness to circumstances, horizontal ("joint") collaboration, and delegation of authority, albeit under political guidance.[10] Notwithstanding the general trend toward increasingly decentralized military C2, U.S. political leaders could be expected to take intense interest in the finest details of Sino-U.S. hostilities, whether or not they would take control of operations.

In contrast to emerging U.S. C2 philosophy, Chinese C2 traditionally emphasizes hierarchy, deference to leaders, reliance on central direction, top-heavy organization, reluctance to delegate authority, and adherence to script.[11] Despite Chinese awareness of the need to loosen up C2 for the sake of agility in the face of uncertainties of war, war control reiterates the need for top-down direction.[12]

---

8   Thom Shanker, "Warning Against Wars Like Iraq and Afghanistan," *The New York Times*, February 25, 2011.

9   Norton A. Schwartz and Jonathan W. Greenert, "Air-Sea Battle: Promoting Stability in an Era of Uncertainty," *The American Interest*, February 20, 2012.

10   See, for example, the seminal work of David Alberts and Richard E. Hayes, *Power to the Edge: Command and Control in the Information Age*, Washington, D.C.: U.S. Department of Defense Command and Control Research Program, 2003. There has also been a reactionary approach to U.S. C2, whereby improved information and communications has given top command the means to exert more, not less, control over operations—the so-called 3,000-mile-long screwdriver micromanagement tendency.

11   Dennis J. Blasko, "The PLA Army/Ground Forces," in Kevin Pollpeter and Kenneth Allen, eds., *The PLA as Organization v2.0*, Vienna, Va.: Defense Group Inc., 2015, p. 260.

12   To date, although there has been a significant change to the PLA *force* structure, there is little evidence to suggest that the *command* and *logistics* structures have adapted to address the more likely combat and nontraditional security contingencies that might occur beyond China's borders and near seas. PLA doctrine foresees many forms of joint campaigns exe-

In tension with the case for tight central control on both sides, military plans and capabilities slant toward a prompt, sharp counterforce exchange, as noted. Both sides are averse to a long war: the Chinese because their prospects decline if and as the United States brings more and more strike-power to bear; the Americans because of their grudging but growing respect for Chinese A2AD capabilities; and both because of the potential military losses and economic costs of prolonged fighting. Yet history shows that war planners tend to claim, and leaders tend to accept, that war will end much sooner than it actually does.[13] As we will see, the more level the battlefield, the longer a Sino-U.S. war could last.

Despite military pressures for a high-intensity conflict, policymakers' doubts about the outcome and fears about the costs could predispose them to try to restrict hostilities. While political control of military operations is more in the Chinese hierarchical C2 style than the American distributed style, leaders of both states could resist appeals to "use or lose" potent but vulnerable forces. While restricted hostilities could be ended readily by leaders determined to minimize losses and avoid escalation, it is also possible that such hostilities could drag on if losses were tolerable and concessions hard.

The less vital the conflict's cause and outcome are to the belligerents, the more inclined and able leaders might be to avoid fierce counterforce exchanges. But war can roil politics, twist psyches, alter stakes,

---

cuted beyond the Chinese mainland that will put naval, air force, or missile units in the lead role. Currently, the existing peacetime chain of command would have to shift to an ad hoc wartime war zone command structure to accommodate the operational changes necessary to accomplish these long-distance joint missions. More-efficient command structures have been discussed in the Chinese military media (mostly talk about flattening the command system), but major changes to the command structure (beyond the reduction of the number of military regions in the 1980s) that was created decades ago in a much different threat environment have yet to be implemented.

[13] Underestimating the duration of conflict was a significant factor in most major strategic blunders of modern times, including Napoleon's invasion of Russia, Germany's decision during World War I to attack neutral shipping, Hitler's invasion of the Soviet Union, Japan's attack on Pearl Harbor, China's invasion of Vietnam, the Soviet invasion of Afghanistan, Argentina's invasion of the Falklands, and the U.S. invasion of Iraq. See Gompert, Binnendijk, and Lin, 2014.

and produce new calculations. Just as the path of war between China and the United States is hard to plan, it is also hard to forecast. For this reason, this study eschews prediction and detailed scenarios in favor of analyzing variables, alternative generic cases suggested by those variables, and consequences of those cases.

Variables of War

Again, a Sino-U.S. conflict can be defined largely by its intensity and duration. While the intensity of fighting could fall anywhere along a continuum, from mild to severe, it suffices for our purposes to analyze the two poles.

Mild connotes tightly restricted operations, in forces committed, weapons used, targets struck, geography, and tempo. Mild conflict might take the form of sporadic fighting, occasional losses, and posturing of forces for advantage, probing, or signaling. Because both Chinese and American forces are capable of fierce warfare, if it is mild, it might be because Chinese and American leaders alike choose it to be. In this case, they are intent on minimizing destruction and avoiding escalation, sparing much of the enemy's targetable forces, even if it means forfeiting a military advantage. Since it would be highly improbable and unstable for one side but not the other to resist counterforce pressure, willingness to do so is presumably communicated, by words or actions, between civilian or military leaders.[14] In effect, a mild conflict implies that the sides *together* try to control a war that neither one, left to itself, can control.

Severe intensity connotes fierce, open-ended operations (short of nuclear war) by each side to gain a decisive advantage by destroying the other side's forces. As already explained, the prospect of such fighting is implied by the fact that both sides have the ability and motivation

---

[14] We do not consider a case in which one side is committed to a mild conflict while the other seeks an intense one. Since both China and the United States are capable of intense fighting, the side that is biased toward restraint must seek to either end the conflict or intensify its attacks.

to conduct conventional counterforce warfare.[15] Severe conflict means that the goal of winning trumps that of limiting the costs of a war. It also implies that each side hopes to weaken the other's will to wage war, which might be less of a consideration if fighting is moderated. All sorts of conventional weapons might be used against whatever military capabilities their sensors can locate and target: moving forces, staging forces, operating bases, logistics flows and infrastructure, air and naval bases, computer networks, satellites, sensors, and military C4ISR. In the future, cyberwarfare against military, dual-purpose, and civilian systems could figure importantly in a severely intense war.

Whether with kinetic or nonkinetic (namely, cyber) weapons, the highest targeting priority for China would be U.S. strike platforms, bases, and force concentrations in the region. For the United States, it would be Chinese A2AD capabilities, mainly located in China. A critical distinction between mild and intense conflict is that the United States would strike targets on Chinese soil in the latter but not the former. Given the improbability that China would sue for peace when attacked on its territory, strikes on the mainland could prolong a severe war.

For analytic purposes, duration could be *brief* or *long*, the former meaning days or weeks and the latter a year or so. Longer wars are also possible but not considered here. Several factors could prolong a Sino-U.S. war: the absence of a clear winner, the determination of both sides to persist in light of the stakes, the results of fighting to that point, the expected results of continued fighting, and the inability to settle on terms of a truce. High military losses and economic costs, as expected in a severe conflict, could either strengthen or weaken resolve, depending on psychological and political factors that are hard to predict. Both sides might opt to pace and restrict operations as a way of conserving their ability to fight, but, again, the urge to use targetable forces against targetable forces could be strong.

While intensity depends on the use and loss of engaged U.S. strike and Chinese A2AD capabilities, the significance of total military

---

[15] As in strategic nuclear theory, counterforce implies an all-out attempt to destroy the other side's forces, which otherwise are sure to be used.

potential, including reinforcements and mobilization capacity, could increase the longer the war's duration. Likewise, economic resilience, political support, and international assistance could affect the ability of one or both sides to continue fighting. Both the United States and China have considerable, if asymmetric, capacity to prolong a conflict that neither one is militarily compelled or politically ready to end.

A critical question is whether one side or the other can achieve such a clear advantage in the early stages of an intense conflict that the other has little choice but to concede. The U.S. ability to achieve such an advantage is declining as China improves its A2AD capabilities. At the same time, China's increasing ability to prevent a decisive, early U.S. advantage does not necessarily translate into its ability to conclude a war quickly on its terms.

Because a mild conflict would place smaller demands on total war-making capacity than a severe one would, it could have a greater potential than the latter to drag on—even becoming a "frozen conflict." Conversely, and obviously, a long, severe conflict would involve greater costs on both sides than other cases in military, economic, and political terms. That a long, severe conflict would be the most costly does not mean it is the least likely. The disposition at any moment to keep fighting depends not only on results, losses, and costs to that point but also on expectations of what is to come. As long as neither side expects to lose, hostilities might continue.

The United States presently has more military capacity than China to wage a long, severe war. For one thing, the United States has substantial forces located in or designated for other regions that it could bring to bear on a conflict in the Western Pacific, though security conditions in those regions might make it reluctant to do so.[16] (Over the years, the Pentagon has crept away from its traditional standard of having sufficient total forces to win two major wars simultane-

---

[16] Although the United States has global responsibilities and interests that could be jeopardized by diverting capabilities to the Asia-Pacific, we assume that the United States would nevertheless commit such capabilities to the theater in the event of a long, severe war with China. Even if another contingency involving U.S. interests developed simultaneously in another region, U.S. forces already in the region could still degrade Chinese A2AD capabilities faster than Chinese A2AD capabilities could degrade U.S. forces.

ously.) Furthermore, U.S. forces today could degrade Chinese A2AD capabilities faster than Chinese A2AD capabilities could degrade U.S. forces. While both might suffer significant losses in early severe hostilities, U.S. prospects currently look better than China's.

Future conditions could differ, owing to the potential for greater losses of U.S. forces from Chinese A2AD and, in turn, reduced Chinese losses from those U.S. forces. Moreover, as U.S. military-operational advantages wane, China's position as the "home team" could become less of a liability and more of an asset, owing to internal lines of communication and movement. A corollary of these shifting military odds is that the expected duration of war, however intense, could *increase* as Chinese capabilities improve, for the simple reason that China will retain more warfighting capability and face less pressure to yield. More generally stated, the less lopsided a war is likely to be, the less likely it is to end quickly in victory by the stronger side. Since Chinese and U.S. capabilities, operating concepts, incentives, and expectations all point to severe hostilities, this could mean that a war could last longer and be costlier than has been assumed or, paradoxically, than either side would want.

The hypothesis of a long, severe, and costly war is depicted in Figure 2.1 as notional graphs of expected cumulative declines, or attrition, in military capability over time in 2015 and 2025, a period during which Chinese A2AD capability is expected to improve relative to U.S. strike capability. The dotted lines in Figure 2.1 represent a hypothetical moment (T_1), within days of the start (T_0), when the sides take stock and decide whether to continue fighting. For our purposes, the figure separates a short conflict from a long one. T_2 is posited as one year; although fighting could continue beyond that, the pattern of losses would remain more or less the same. The first graph (2015) shows that China and the United States both suffer significant but unequal losses in the brief early stage and can expect increasingly divergent losses as war goes on, favoring the United States. The second (2025) shows the effects of improved Chinese A2AD in years to come: China suffers reduced, though still sizable, short-term losses; the United States suffers increased short-term losses; and the gap in expected long-term losses closes.

Figure 2.1
Notional Cumulative Decline in Military Capabilities in a Severe Conflict over Time, 2015 and 2025

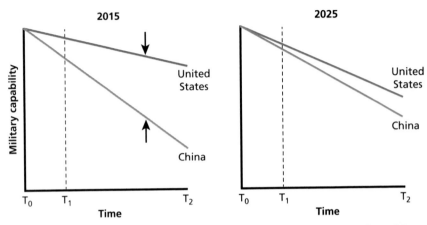

NOTES: T_0 = the start of the conflict; T_1 = a hypothetical moment, within days of T_0, when the sides decide whether to continue fighting; T_2 = one year.

RAND RR1140-2.1

The intensity and duration of war are largely decided at T_0 and T_1, respectively. The moment hostilities begin, Chinese and U.S. leaders choose whether or not to authorize execution of military plans, which are mainly to attack the forces of the other before those forces can attack. The alternative is to decide, mutually, that fighting must be tightly controlled and sharply restricted—in other words, mild. Thus, the T_0 decision might determine the war's intensity, which in these graphs is assumed to be severe from T_0 to T_2. At T_1, after several days of severe force-on-force violence, the leaders take stock of losses, remaining capabilities, and expected further losses and decide whether to keep fighting—in effect, they choose between a short and a long war. Again, a decision by only one side to end fighting amounts to capitulation. Note that China's enhanced A2AD in 2025 will reduce the gap between its losses and U.S. losses at T_1. Because it could be less clear which side is losing at T_1, a severe war might be more likely to be prolonged in 2025 than in 2015, despite mounting costs.

These considerations highlight the fallacy of assuming that particularly violent hostilities would not last long (as European leaders did in 1914!). Again, the Chinese have favored and planned for a brief, intense war because they think it is the only way not to lose. However, this perspective ignores that the United States is looking at a mirror image: After brief and intense fighting, U.S. *prospective* losses will be less than those of China. Yet if the United States has until now thought that an intense war would be short because Chinese losses would exceed U.S. losses by a growing margin as fighting persists, it should think again.

Going forward, both China and the United States need to contemplate the possibility of a severe, lengthy, uncontrollable, and devastating, yet indecisive, conflict. If war somehow broke out and both sides faced such prospects, they would not necessarily be motivated to stop fighting by agreement. History offers little encouragement that opponents locked in a bloody but inconclusive war will agree to foreshorten it, rational as that might be.[17] Therefore, the potential automaticity and instability inherent in conventional counterforce places an onus on political leaders to review, question, approve, and reexamine warfighting plans.

Depending on choices made by political leaders among options offered by military commanders, either a short war or a lengthy one could be intense or mild; we examine all four cases. At the same time, it seems more likely that a long but mild conflict would result more from initially mild fighting than from initially intense fighting and, conversely, that intense fighting will remain intense as long as the war lasts. After all, both world wars started with ferocity, which persisted and even intensified more or less for their durations. Of course, it cannot be ruled out that a war could begin fiercely but then settle into a low-grade one, as both sides conclude they cannot win, refuse to concede, and try to moderate their losses.

One of the most vexing trade-offs leaders face in determining how intensely and how long to fight is between the cost of fighting and the

---

[17] By 1917, the combination of staggering losses and diminished confidence of victory led voices in Germany, Great Britain, and France to suggest the need to negotiate, but both sides opted to fight on (until the U.S. entry into the war decided the outcome).

cost of losing. The former will tend to motivate restricting the conflict even if it means forfeiting advantage; the latter will tend to motivate doing what it takes to win, including intensifying, expanding, and prolonging the conflict. To illustrate, the United States might feel reasonably confident that it could win in an intense war with China yet face such severe costs that it might rather keep the war limited and accept an outcome short of victory, though presumably consistent with U.S. interests. Conversely, China might regard the price of losing a war with the United States over, say, Taiwan as so high that it would endure the costs of an intense, and perhaps lengthy, conflict. Broadly speaking, as prospects of either side clearly winning decline, as might be the case in coming years, both sides ought to place greater weight on the costs of fighting—a key reason why both must rigorously think through what consequences a war could have.

The costs of a conflict are mainly a function of intensity and duration.[18] Least costly, obviously, is a brief, mild war; most costly, a long, severe one. The kinds of costs vary over time: Initially, military losses will dominate; in time, economic costs will grow, and military losses might decline as counterforce capabilities do. Domestic political constraints and pressures might be in play from the outset, but these, too, could gain strength and even sway leaders' choices as military losses and economic costs mount. Likewise, international reactions and uncertainties—alarm, condemnation, opposition, political support, physical support, and realignments—might grow over time and with severity.

Using duration and intensity as the main variables in describing the path of war suggests a matrix of four cases: *brief, mild*; *long, mild*; *brief, severe*; and *long, severe*. (Other possibilities are not examined but could be interpolated.) The assumptions for each case are shown in Table 2.1.

---

[18] The costs of war also vary as a function of the vulnerability of the combatants. In the case of a Sino-U.S. war, forces in the theater are increasingly vulnerable, and dependence on global (including each other's) resources, products, and markets makes both economies vulnerable. However, China would be far more exposed to homeland attack and economic isolation.

Table 2.1
Matrix of the Four Cases

	Brief	Long
Mild	**Premise:** Leaders restrict hostilities and quickly agree to end conflict. **Description:** • Hostilities are triggered by incident or miscalculation, possibly involving a third party. • Political leaders take immediate and tight control of operations, communicate directly, withhold authority for major attacks on opposing forces, and agree to end conflict with no change in the status quo. • Hostilities end within a week or so.	**Premise:** Leaders restrict hostilities but do not agree to end conflict. **Description:** • This is an extension of the brief, mild case. • Political control keeps hostilities limited. • Forces of both sides are augmented and operate in close proximity. Incidents and losses are sporadic but continue. • Leaders communicate but cannot agree on terms to end fighting. • Low-grade conflict is economically and politically sustainable, as neither side wants to concede or to wage costly war. • Conflict persists for a year or more.
Severe	**Premise:** War-winning logic and counterforce strategies govern from the outset. **Description:** • Stakes are very important for both sides. • Crisis becomes unstable because of counterforce pressures. • Military concept of operations executed immediately by both sides. China uses kill chain to attack U.S. aircraft carriers and air bases. Simultaneously, U.S. attacks kill chain. • There are selective U.S. strikes on China. • Both sides wage selective cyberwar. • Military-operational exigencies dictate fast pace and severe intensity. • Political leaders get control only by agreeing on terms to end conflict. • Conflict lasts a week or so.	**Premise:** Severe fighting persists per war-winning logic, absence of clear winner, deepened antagonism, and strengthened resolve. **Description:** • Leaders cannot or choose not to stop. • Losses make compromise harder, not easier. • Extensive U.S. strikes on China. • Nonnuclear escalation occurs: geographically, and with respect to targets, weapons, expanded cyberwar, and ASAT. • Both sides face continued high losses. • Both sides bring more forces into action; China mobilizes for long war as losses mount. • Conflict persists for a year or more.

Note once again that the main factor in determining whether a war is restrained or severe from the outset is whether political leaders give their militaries the green light for counterforce attacks. One can speculate on both institutional and rational-choice grounds whether restraint would be exercised. U.S. civilian control of the military is firm in principle and practice. Though the current Chinese president has felt a need to tighten control over the PLA, little information is available to assess how current Chinese civilian and military leaders would handle command authority during wartime. Even with adequate institutional safeguards on both sides, the logic of striking without delay is potent. Because hesitation could result in operational losses and disadvantages too great to overcome, the "safe" course might be to strike enemy forces promptly, if not first.

Note also that lower stakes and inadvertent violence are less likely to precipitate severe hostilities than higher stakes and a considered choice of war are. Furthermore, a long conflict will likely conform to the level of intensity established at its outset. In the severe case, though costs are great on both sides, neither one is likely to have clearly better prospects. Also, if the stakes are important, high losses can work against rather than for accommodation and cessation. Even if fighting is restricted and sporadic, its continuation might appear less costly, at least politically, than conceding the matter at hand.

Upper and Lower Limits

Before estimating the possible losses, costs, and other effects of these four cases, it is worth considering the lower and upper limits of a war's severity.

One can easily imagine a conflict between China and the United States below the threshold of what has been described here as "mild." Just as Russia has used nonviolent means, along with some violent ones (e.g., so-called little green men) to intervene in and carve out chunks of Ukraine, China has and uses an array of military and nonmilitary means to advance its interests at the expense of its neighbors and of the United States. Indeed, China is pursuing such a strategy (*sans* little green men) to press its sweeping territorial claims in the East China and South China Seas: interfering with other states' vessels, placing oil rigs and artificial islands in disputed waters, and menacingly reminding neighbors that "China is a big country and other countries are small countries, and that's just a fact."[19] Clearly, the Chinese seek to isolate and pressure neighbors without triggering U.S. intervention. Just as clearly, the United States and its allies, including Japan, can and will engage in reciprocal actions.[20] To the extent both China and the United States are involved, one can see a sort of conflict that is short of violent use of force. U.S. strategy to thwart such a Chinese campaign is important but not germane to this study. Although the costs and consequences of such "gray area" conflict would be even lower than those of a mild armed conflict, as defined earlier, there is some possibility that regional commerce could suffer as a result.

At the other extreme, the long, severe case is not necessarily the upper limit of what war could entail and cost. The United States and China are the world's strongest nations, with the largest economies, two of the three biggest populations, vast human and natural resources, and unsurpassed war-making capacity. While the two countries have important convergent peacetime interests, there is also considerable "strategic distrust" between them.[21] Should they go to war, distrust could turn to deep antagonism, and the logic of conflict could make possible levels of violence, duration, and cost that might appear unjustifiable in times of peace. In modern history, wars involving great and more or less evenly matched powers have sucked in numerous third parties (not just prewar allies), lasted years, metastasized to other regions, and forced belligerents to shift their economies to a war footing and their societies to a war psyche. Whole populations suspend

---

[19] Chinese Foreign Minister Yang Jiechi's quoted in John Pomfret, "U.S. Takes a Tougher Tone with China," *The Washington Post*, July 30, 2010.

[20] In their bilateral security consultations, the Japanese and Americans have identified Chinese "gray area" aggression as contingencies that require heightened attention and joint planning.

[21] The apt term *strategic distrust* was coined in Kenneth Lieberthal and Wang Jisi, *Addressing U.S.-Chinese Strategic Distrust*, Washington, D.C.: John L. Thornton China Center, Brookings Institution, 2012.

normal life; large fractions of them are prepared or forced to throw their weight behind their nation's fight. Not just states but opposing ideologies, worldviews, and political systems might be pitted against each other. Whatever their initial causes, such wars' outcomes might determine which great powers and their blocs survive as such. Prewar international systems collapse or are transformed to serve the victors' interests. Thus, the costs of failing outweigh those of fighting.

Consider how the Napoleonic wars engulfed all of Europe, how World War I destroyed several empires and enlarged others, and how allied goals in World War II became the complete destruction of German fascism and Japanese militarism, rather than merely stopping their aggression. In such cases, war aims and acts of destruction might exceed belligerents' early intentions by a wide margin. Regimes of the losing side usually vanish. The threshold of tolerable costs might rise as fighting persists and the penalty for losing increases. There have been exceptions: Prussia's victories in the three wars of German unification and the American victory over Spain come to mind. But these were one-sided affairs between mismatched powers ending quickly and decisively, without spreading or drawing in other powers.

Would a war between China and the United States resemble the great-power wars of modern history—expansive, systemic, desperate? Would hostilities erase all residue of mutual interest in an international order that has served both countries well? Would the escalating costs of conflict seem tolerable compared with those of losing? Would the enemy be demonized? Would populations become targets?

The only honest answer to such questions is that no one knows. As we will see, the increasing probability of inconclusive hostilities between China and the United States might suggest a bias toward a long, severe, bitter war. Moreover, it cannot be excluded that such a Sino-U.S. war could develop characteristics of the two great-power wars that became "world wars": drawing in others, engulfing and spilling beyond the region, locking the two political systems and populations into a fight to finish, ending in unconditional surrender, dictated peace, occupation, regime extinction, and domination.

At the same time, the expansion and immense destructiveness of modern great-power wars have resulted mainly from large and ferocious land campaigns and strategic bombing, aimed at conquest. Although one cannot rule it out, such war aims and fighting seem unlikely in even a major Sino-U.S. war unless it stemmed from miscalculations during a conflict on the Korean peninsula. Moreover, the United States would restrain, if not avoid, strategic bombing of China lest it precipitate nuclear war. Having said this, it could be that the long, severe case offered here for analytic purposes might not set the upper limit of a possible war between China and the United States.

The possibility of a long and severe war, in which willingness to accept hardship and to inflict harm grows as fighting lasts, returns us to the question of whether such a war might result in the use of nuclear weapons. We assess the probability of that to be very low and so do not include the effects of nuclear warfare in our analysis of losses and costs.[22] The general reason for this is that *mutual deterrence* prevails in the Sino-U.S. strategic-nuclear relationship.[23]

Nonetheless, it is worth examining the circumstances in which the risk of nuclear war, however low, could be at its highest. In a prolonged and severe conflict, it is conceivable that Chinese military leaders would propose and Chinese political leaders would consider using nuclear weapons in the following circumstances:

- Chinese forces are at risk of being totally destroyed.
- The Chinese homeland has been rendered defenseless against U.S. conventional attacks; such attacks are extensive and go beyond military targets, perhaps to include political leadership.
- Domestic economic and political conditions are growing so dire that the state itself could collapse.
- U.S. conventional strikes include or are perceived to include capabilities that are critical to China's strategic deterrent—notably intercontinental ballistic missile (ICBMs), ballistic missile sub-

---

[22] Obviously, losses and costs to both countries in the event of nuclear war could be at least an order of magnitude greater than the worst of the conventional-war cases examined here.

[23] The stability of the Sino-U.S. nuclear relationship is explained in Chapter Four of David C. Gompert and Phillip C. Saunders, *The Paradox of Power: Sino-American Strategic Restraint in an Age of Vulnerability*, Washington, D.C.: Center for the Study of Chinese Military Affairs, National Defense University, 2011.

marines (SSBNs), strategic C2—which the Chinese interpret as preparation for a U.S. first strike or intended to leave China vulnerable to U.S. nuclear coercion.

Thus, it cannot be entirely excluded that the Chinese leadership would decide that *only* the use of nuclear weapons would prevent total defeat and the state's destruction. However, even under such desperate conditions, the resort to nuclear weapons would not be China's only option: It could instead accept defeat. Indeed, because U.S. nuclear retaliation would make the destruction of the state and collapse of the country all the more certain, accepting defeat would be a better option (depending on the severity of U.S. terms) than nuclear escalation. This logic, along with China's ingrained no-first-use policy, suggests that Chinese first use is most improbable.[24]

At the same time, if Chinese leaders faced such a dire situation *and* also had reason to think that the United States was preparing to launch a first strike to disable China's deterrent, they might consider the first use of nuclear weapons (even though, objectively, it might not be rational). But this also seems like an extremely remote possibility for the simple reason that the United States would have no reason to resort to nuclear weapons if it were already on the verge of conventional victory over China.

Even so, it is important for the United States to be aware of potentially dangerous ambiguities involved in attacks on targets that the Chinese could regard as strategic: attacks on missile launchers, even if intended only to degrade China's theater-range missile capabilities; attacks on high-level military C2, even if intended only to degrade China's conventional-operational capabilities; cyberwarfare attacks on strategic systems; attacks on Beijing (whatever the reason); and heightened U.S. ballistic missile defense operations that could be seen as intended to degrade Chinese strategic retaliation. Keep in mind, as well, that the Chinese might perceive U.S. conventional capabilities

---

[24] As a corollary, if China were to use nuclear weapons first, it could be a "warning shot"—a relatively harmless detonation in a remote area—as opposed to nuclear attack on U.S. forces, territory, or allies.

(e.g., global strike, cyberwarfare, ASAT) as potentially aimed at disabling China's strategic deterrent.

As low as the probability of Chinese first use is, even in the most desperate circumstances of a prolonged and severe war, the United States could make it lower still by exercising great care with regard to the extensiveness of homeland attacks and by avoiding altogether targets that the Chinese could interpret as critical to their deterrent.

As for U.S. initiation of nuclear war with China, this seems even more far-fetched. Unlike circumstances in which the Soviet Union could not be stopped from defeating NATO and dominating all of Europe unless the United States resorted to battlefield nuclear weapons, the stakes of a Sino-U.S. war would not justify the incalculable harm to the United States from Chinese retaliation. More bluntly put, the Soviet threat to NATO was deemed existential, whereas as the Chinese threat to U.S. allies and interests in East Asia is not. In line with this, current U.S. declaratory policy concerning use of nuclear weapons makes no allowance for first-use in the event of war with China, even were it going badly.[25]

In sum, it seems unlikely that war between China and the United States would "go global," or "go nuclear." In either case, the losses, costs, and other consequences for both and the world would dwarf those estimated for a severe and prolonged conventional conflict in the Western Pacific. Still, the possibility of a true cataclysm is all the more reason to think through carefully the paths and risks of war.

---

[25] U.S. policy reserves the option of nuclear first use mainly in retaliation for a biological attack.

CHAPTER THREE

Weighing the Costs: Military, Economic, Political, and International

With the understanding that the consequences of world war and of nuclear war fall outside our scope, we can now examine possible effects, losses, costs, constraints, pressures, and responses that could occur during Sino-U.S. war, depending on its severity and duration.

Military Losses

Calculating expected military losses in a Sino-U.S. armed conflict is exceedingly difficult. For purposes of understanding the major issues surrounding whether and how such a conflict might be fought, it is sufficient to estimate *indicatively* the nature and seriousness of losses of each side, how they might compare, how they might vary according to the severity and duration of the conflict, and how they might affect decisionmaking on both sides. Accordingly, the method used here is to meld the broad judgments of several analysts.[1] Of interest are losses relative to prewar capabilities, losses of each side compared with the other, and residual warfighting capabilities, all of which would bear on both the ability and will to continue fighting.

---

[1] The judgments here are informed by the Sino-U.S. conflict scenarios from RAND Arroyo Center research by Terrence K. Kelly, David C. Gompert, and Duncan Long, which will be presented in *Smarter Power, Stronger Partners: Exploiting U.S. Advantages to Prevent Aggression*, Santa Monica, Calif.: RAND Corporation, RR-1359-A, forthcoming.

Severe cases for both 2015 and 2025 are considered, anticipating Chinese A2AD improvements.[2] Losses in brief conflicts (up to T_1) are among forces engaged and targetable from the outset. Additional losses in prolonged conflicts (from T_1 to T_2) could include reinforcements—perhaps nearly all extant Chinese air and naval forces and those U.S. air and naval forces not deemed indispensable for missions elsewhere (e.g., in Europe or the Middle East).

Prospective losses in forces during a severe Sino-U.S. conflict would depend on the counterforce capabilities and operations of the two sides, of course. To expand on an earlier observation, advances in information technology and other targeting systems—sensors, onboard and off-board precision weapon guidance, global positioning, and data networking and processing—are making weapon platforms, such as surface ships and manned aircraft, increasingly vulnerable at greater distances. In addition to increasing the reward of attacking first and the penalty of not doing so, these capabilities point to the potential for heavier, faster losses among vulnerable forces than at any time in modern conventional warfare.[3]

The assessments that follow try to capture this dynamic. They include broad-brush narratives of the cases and graphs that illustratively depict losses. The categories covered include combat aircraft, surface naval vessels, submarines, missiles and missile launchers of all types (land, sea, and air), and C4ISR. Aircraft losses could result from loss or degradation of air bases and aircraft carriers, as well as air combat and air defense. Surface ship losses could result from attacks by other surface ships, submarines, air, or missile attacks. Submarines are vulnerable to anti-submarine warfare (ASW), including opposing submarines, and strikes on bases. Losses in missile launchers could occur from air or missile strikes or destroyed platforms (e.g., ships), as well as from missiles expended. Mobile land-based missile launchers, which Chinese forces possess in greater abundance than U.S. forces, might

---

[2]   U.S. force improvements are assumed to be those provided for in the exiting long-range U.S. defense program.

[3]   This counterforce phenomenon does not apply to cyberwarfare or ASAT warfare, in which attacks do not diminish the other side's capability to attack.

be less vulnerable. C4ISR losses could result from cyberwar or ASAT attacks. Cyberwar and ASAT attacks could also compound losses of forces that depend on C4ISR for their effectiveness. Additional details are in Appendix A.

An important consideration in estimating U.S. losses and comparing them with Chinese losses is the share of total (global) U.S. forces engaged. The greater that share, the better the United States would do militarily. However, committing more U.S. forces to the theater would also increase those that are targetable and vulnerable to Chinese A2AD. Very broadly speaking, more U.S. forces would mean a larger and more violent war, with higher losses on both sides but higher expectations of U.S. victory. The share of U.S. forces committed would be determined by trading off the demands of the war against the effect on security in other regions of diverting U.S. forces. The latter, in turn, could be affected by the extent to which U.S. allies, notably NATO, could "cover" for the diversion of U.S. forces elsewhere. Our main interest is in naval, air, land-based missile, air-defense, and intelligence, surveillance, and reconnaissance (ISR) capabilities, since Sino-U.S. war presumably would not involve large land combat. The U.S. Department of Defense has said that 60 percent of U.S. air and naval forces will be based in the Pacific by 2020.[4] Accordingly, the assumption here is that in the course of a prolonged war with China, the United States would commit 60 percent of its global capabilities; U.S. military losses are estimated relative to that. If the figure were higher in the event, losses on both sides could increase.

Table 3.1 provides estimates of military losses for cases of severe fighting for one year, more or less. It is assumed that cases of tightly restricted fighting would involve minor and roughly equivalent military losses.

Estimated losses can be presented graphically, similar to the earlier graphs of hypothetical losses in 2015 and 2025. Figure 3.1 shows *aggregate* cumulative losses, with graphs for each of the force categories discussed in Appendix A. Losses are shown from top to bottom, start-

---

[4]   Robert Work, Deputy Secretary of Defense, statement to the Council of Foreign Relations, January 20, 2015.

Table 3.1
Estimated Military Losses, Severe Case, 2015

Capability	U.S. Losses	Chinese Losses
Air forces	Some possibility of early loss of a carrier to Chinese submarines or missiles and of use of regional air bases to missiles. Significant aircraft losses to Chinese surface-to-air missiles until suppressed.	Sharp loss of air power from U.S. air strikes, air intercept, and air defense. Reinforcements are less capable and more vulnerable. China can keep some aircraft hidden but out of use.
Surface naval forces	Significant early losses of forward fleet because of submarine and missile attacks. Losses can be limited by keeping fleet out of range, or out of effective use. Strikes on Chinese anti-naval forces reduce U.S. losses in time.	Heavy initial and sustained fleet losses because of U.S. air power and submarines. Naval bases vulnerable. Chinese shipbuilding capacity only takes effect in the long term (post-T_2) and is vulnerable.
Submarines	Largely invulnerable to poor and quickly depleted Chinese ASW capability.	Older submarines vulnerable to U.S. ASW. A few advanced ones survive and threaten U.S. surface forces.
Missile launchers (land, surface, submarine, air) and missile inventories	Surface ship-launch and short-range air-launch platforms suffer attrition. Submarine-launch and long-range air-launch survive. Major expenditure of missiles.	Land launchers survive if mobile or hidden. U.S. air power and missiles eventually wear down Chinese missile launchers. Also susceptible to degraded C4ISR. Large fraction of modern missiles expended early, leaving older, less accurate shorter-range ones.
C4ISR (computer systems and satellites)	Some loss because of Chinese cyberwar and ASAT, which are difficult to suppress.	Some loss because of U.S. cyberwar and ASAT capabilities. Also, untested C2 processes could unravel under pressure of war.
Aggregate	Chinese counterforce capabilities take a major early toll on the United States but then have less of an effect as they are degraded by superior U.S. counterforce.	U.S. counterforce capabilities take a major toll early and throughout as Chinese A2AD is degraded.

Figure 3.1
Estimated Aggregate Loss in Military Capability, Severe Case, 2015

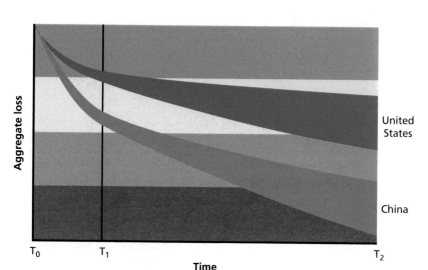

NOTES: Losses are shown from top to bottom, starting with full capabilities when the war begins. The green band signifies modest losses; yellow, significant losses; orange, heavy losses; and red, very heavy losses.
RAND *RR1140-3.1*

ing with full capabilities when the war begins. The green band signifies modest losses; yellow, significant losses; orange, heavy losses; and red, very heavy losses.[5]

Illustratively, each band might be thought of as roughly a tenth or so of effective capabilities committed. These estimates are based on raw judgments of several analysts, rather than on calculations predicated on detailed war games or computer simulations. The width of the curves signifies uncertainty, which increases the longer fighting lasts.

Note that China would suffer significantly greater losses than the United States by T_1, as its weapons are expended and its platforms and bases are struck. Thereafter, as more U.S. strike power is committed and Chinese defenses are degraded, the differential in losses contin-

---

[5] Depending on the category, decline in effective capabilities could be measured in ships or aircraft lost, in missiles used or destroyed, or in the degradation of C4ISR performance because of loss of space assets or networks.

ues or expands. Though large, this gap has been reduced by Chinese deployment of advanced A2AD capabilities, prompting the U.S. military to consider striking those capabilities, which are mainly on Chinese territory.

At present, if the United States were to discount the risk of escalation and unleash its strike power at the stroke of T_0, Chinese losses at T_1 and beyond could be even greater than shown in the figure. Likewise, China might be able to reduce the gap in losses at T_1 and beyond by attacking U.S. strike forces preemptively. The potential difference in losses depending on which side strikes first (though not shown graphically) underscores the instability inherent in counterforce capabilities and concepts on both sides.

Presumably, China would be as aware as the United States that the gap in losses at T_1 would keep growing in a prolonged war (as shown). Using our scale, the decline in Chinese capabilities (as defined earlier) by T_2 could be extremely heavy, whereas U.S. losses could be significant but less heavy. Apart from a preemptive attack on U.S. forces, China's best chance, though perhaps not a very good one, is to seek a quick end to severe fighting. The wide gap in losses from outset to finish suggests that Chinese planning for a short war is wishful, perhaps based on a belief that the United States would not have the stomach to fight after suffering significant losses (which would be a misreading of the history of U.S. war making).[6]

By 2025, China will likely have more, better, and longer-range ballistic missiles and cruise missiles; advanced air defenses; latest-generation aircraft; quieter submarines; more and better sensors; and the digital communications, processing power, and C2 necessary to operate an integrated kill chain. The United States, it is assumed here, will have modernized versions of the platform-centric force-projection capabilities on which it has relied for some decades, despite their growing vulnerability to Chinese A2AD. Prospective losses in a severe war would change accordingly, as shown in Table 3.2 and Figure 3.2.

---

[6]   Think of World War II (after Pearl Harbor), the Korean War, the Vietnam War, and the recent wars in Iraq and Afghanistan.

Table 3.2
Estimated Military Losses, Severe Case, 2025

Capability	U.S. Losses	Chinese Losses
Air forces	Early and subsequent loss of carriers to submarines and missiles. Degraded use of regional air bases because of missile attack. Aircraft losses to improved Chinese air defense and air force.	U.S. air power losses improve survivability of Chinese air power. China has more-advanced aircraft and improved refueling. Losses are still substantial.
Surface naval forces	Major losses early and throughout from improved Chinese submarines, missiles, and air power. Somewhat mitigated by increased weapon ranges.	Marginally less vulnerable because of degraded U.S. sea and air power. U.S. submarines cause major losses.
Submarines	Somewhat more vulnerable to improved Chinese ASW.	More-advanced submarines are less vulnerable to ASW than older ones.
Missile launchers (land, surface, submarine, air) and missile inventories	Increased vulnerability of surface-naval and air-launch platforms. Large missile expenditures starting early and throughout.	Reduced vulnerability of launchers to U.S. air and missile attacks. Increased numbers and sophistication. Large expenditures early and throughout.
C4ISR (computer systems and satellites)	Sharp initial and sustained degradation from improved Chinese cyberwar and ASAT capabilities.	Sharp initial and sustained degradation from improved U.S. cyberwar and ASAT capabilities.
Aggregate	Improved and less vulnerable Chinese A2AD produces increased U.S. losses early and throughout.	Increased loss of U.S. strike forces could reduce losses of Chinese forces, though still greater than U.S. losses early and throughout.

Improved Chinese A2AD would increase losses of U.S. strike forces, which in turn might lower Chinese losses. Note especially that while the United States would still have an advantage at T_1, it could be less pronounced. Because actual losses at T_1 and expected losses thereafter do not indicate a clear winner, there could be a greater inclination on both sides to continue hostilities. If so, the gap between U.S. and Chinese losses could be smaller in 2025 than in 2015, and could even

Figure 3.2
Estimated Aggregate Loss in Military Capability, Severe Case, 2025

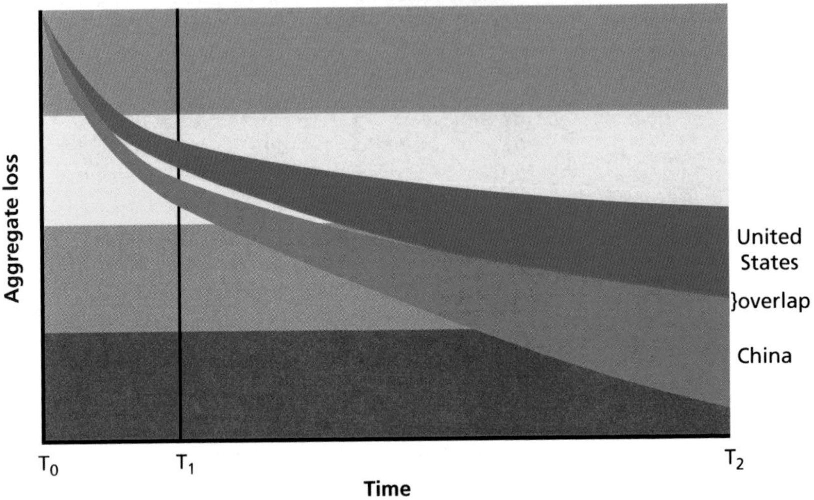

NOTES: Losses are shown from top to bottom, starting with full capabilities when the war begins. The green band signifies modest losses; yellow, significant losses; orange, heavy losses; and red, very heavy losses.
RAND RR1140-3.2

shrink after T_1. The overlap of the loss curves by T_2 indicates that the United States might not be able to gain a decisive military-operational advantage in 2025 even with the prolongation of fighting.

Apart from the gap between them, note that U.S. and Chinese military losses in a long, severe 2025 war would both be very heavy—U.S. losses because of China's improved A2AD, and China's losses despite its improved A2AD. By T_2, Chinese losses could remain very heavy, whereas U.S. losses in the region could be heavy (notably, heavier than in 2015). This implies a sizable depletion in overall U.S. military capabilities and an even larger depletion in overall Chinese military capabilities, with implications for postwar security in this and other regions. Yet with no clear winner, neither side able to gain control, and heavy losses causing deep anger on both sides, prospects for agreement to foreshorten the war could be lower than they are now.

Economic Costs

Owing to the size, interdependence, and global integration of the U.S. and Chinese economies, a Sino-U.S. war could be immensely costly for the belligerents, East Asia, and the world. These vulnerabilities are a major reason why war, at least a premeditated one, is so unlikely, even though the two states are and likely will remain at odds over a number of regional disputes. Should a war nevertheless occur (perhaps from a mismanaged crisis), the scale of economic costs would depend on its severity and duration. In contrast to military losses, even a mild level of hostilities, if prolonged, could inflict serious economic harm. But the focus here is on the economic effects of severe hostilities.

Estimating economic costs of a Sino-U.S. war is, if anything, more difficult than estimating military losses, for such costs depend not only on military developments but also on the response of sundry economic actors and markets with limited degrees of state control: government policy responses, possible economic warfare, the fate of industrial enterprises, the effect on and reactions of consumers and workers, international financial institutions, debt and equity markets, and third parties (i.e., trading partners). Accordingly, the analysis that follows is meant not to be definitive but instead illustrative of the sorts and scale of costs in the different cases.

To summarize current economic conditions:

- China's GDP is about $9 trillion and has been growing at 7 percent annually, although many economists believe that growth will slow, and some argue that growth rates are exaggerated.[7]

---

[7] International Monetary Fund, *World Economic Outlook Database*, October 2014. For more information about projections of future growth and the accuracy of reported growth rates, see Center for Strategic and International Studies, "Long-Term Growth Rates: Can China Maintain Its Current Growth?" Washington, D.C., October 2009; Bob Davis, "China Growth Seen Slowing Sharply over Decade," *The Wall Street Journal*, October 20, 2014; Yukon Huang, "China's Misleading Economic Indicators," *Financial Times*, August 29, 2014; and Derek Scissors, "China's Real GDP [Growth] Is Slower Than Official Figures Show," *Financial Times*, January 20, 2015.

- U.S. GDP is about $17 trillion and is growing at 2 percent annually.[8]
- China's exports to the United States were about $440 billion in 2013—roughly 20 percent of U.S. imports, 20 percent of Chinese exports, and 5 percent of China's GDP.[9]
- China's imports from the United States were about $122 billion in 2013—roughly 6 percent of Chinese imports, 8 percent of U.S. exports, and under 1 percent of U.S. GDP.[10]
- China holds about $1.7 trillion in U.S. securities, including about $1.3 trillion in U.S. Treasury bonds—about 25 percent of all U.S. Treasury debt held by foreign countries.[11]
- Total Chinese direct investment in the U.S. is roughly $8 billion, compared with total U.S. direct investment in China of over $60 billion.[12]
- International trade is about 45 percent of China's GDP and 25 percent of U.S. GDP.
- Chinese consumption is one-third of GDP (and climbing); U.S. consumption is two-thirds of GDP.[13]

Key asymmetries include China's greater reliance on international trade in general (especially with regard to energy supplies), reliance on exports to the United States in particular, and holdings of U.S. debt; U.S. reliance on imports from China; U.S. direct investment in China; and higher U.S. consumption as share of GDP. In considering the eco-

---

[8] International Monetary Fund, 2014.

[9] U.S. Census Bureau, "2013: U.S. Trade in Goods with China," 2013; World Trade Organization, "China," trade profile, September 2014.

[10] U.S. Census Bureau, 2013.

[11] U.S. Department of the Treasury, Federal Reserve Bank of New York, and Board of Governors of the Federal Reserve System, *Foreign Portfolio Holdings of U.S. Securities*, April 2014.

[12] U.S. Bureau of Economic Analysis, "Balance of Payments and Direct Investment Position Data (U.S. Direct Investment Position Abroad on a Historical-Cost Basis and Foreign Direct Investment Position in the United States on a Historical-Cost Basis)," n.d.

[13] World Bank, "Household Final Consumption Expenditure, etc. (% of GDP)," World Development Indicators, 2014b.

nomic costs of war, perhaps the most significant asymmetry is that intensive and extensive combat in the Western Pacific would disrupt nearly *all* Chinese trade (95 percent of it being seaborne), whereas the United States would mainly suffer the loss of bilateral trade with China and, to a much lesser extent than China, trade with the rest of East Asia.[14] This might be thought of as the *war-zone effect* on trade.

This particular asymmetry between China and the United States is depicted in concentric circles in Figure 3.3. The center circles represent *bilateral (Sino-U.S.) trade,* the middle circles represent *other regional trade,* and the outer circles represent *other global trade.* The percentages shown in each circle indicate the share of that country's global trade. The depiction is intended as impressionistic, not to exact

Figure 3.3
Illustrative War-Zone Effect on Trade

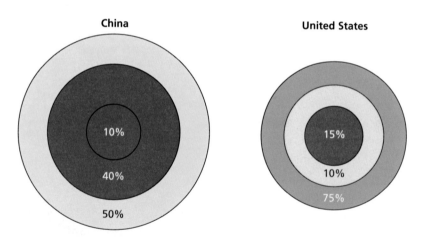

NOTES: The center circles represent bilateral (Sino-U.S.) trade, the middle circles represent other regional trade, and the outer circles represent other global trade. The percentages shown in each circle indicate the share of that country's global trade. The difference in size represents China's greater dependence on trade. Red indicates extreme vulnerability of trade in the event of a major war; yellow, significant vulnerability; and green, minor vulnerability.
RAND RR1140-3.3

---

[14] China's access to the rest of East Asia would be affected much more than would U.S. access.

scale. The difference in size represents China's greater dependence on trade than the United States.

The figure also shows the potential vulnerability of trade in the event of war. Red indicates the extreme vulnerability of trade in the event of a major war; yellow, significant vulnerability; and green, minor vulnerability.

Thus, China's bilateral trade with the United States and other regional trade could be extremely vulnerable, whereas for the United States, only trade with China would be greatly affected. Overall, most of China's trade (except for the small overland fraction) is vulnerable to disruptions in seaborne trade in the Western Pacific, whereas most U.S. trade is not.[15] This, as we will see, has asymmetric effects on GDP in the event of war.

The vulnerability of Chinese trade begs a further question: Would the United States forcibly blockade nonmilitary sea and air transport to and from China? Keep in mind that both sides have large arrays of capabilities to destroy ships and aircraft—anti-surface and anti-air missiles, air strike power, submarines, and surface-naval strike power, not to mention cyberwar—as well as incentives to use them. Also, while the United States has sophisticated sensors to distinguish military from nonmilitary targets, during war it will focus on finding and tracking the former; moreover, Chinese ISR is less sophisticated and discriminating, especially at a distance. This suggests very hazardous airspace and sea space, perhaps ranging from the Yellow Sea to the South China Sea. Assuming that non-Chinese commercial enterprises would rather lose revenue than ships or planes, the United States would not *need* to use force to stop trade to and from China.[16] China would lose a substantial amount of trade that would be required to transit the war zone. The United States expressly threatening commercial shipping would be

---

[15] China could expand its overland trade during a war, especially with Russia. But that would hardly make a dent in China's loss of access to the rest of the world for markets, capital goods, and materials.

[16] The United States could inflict significant damage on Chinese shipping, as it has done in previous severe conflicts against other countries. For example, U.S. submarines exacted tremendous losses on Japanese shipping vessels in World War II; these losses were arguably critical to Japan's economic collapse during the war.

provocative, hazardous, and largely unnecessary. So we posit no U.S. blockade, as such.

The analysis that follows assumes severe fighting, the duration of which (from T_0 to T_1 to T_2) would determine the magnitude of economic effects. Rough costs are estimated in terms of effect on GDP from disruptions of three economic functions: trade, consumption, and income from overseas investments. The effects of energy-supply disruption to China are considered as a component of the contraction in trade, because most natural gas and crude oil consumed by China are imported. It is assumed that the current conditions, importance, and relationships of the U.S. and Chinese economies will not change in character by 2025 (unlike expected changes in military capabilities over that time).[17]

Only direct GDP losses are considered; no attempt has been made to estimate the effect of war on the regional and global economies and, in turn, the rebound impacts on the U.S. and Chinese economies. Also not included are costs with little immediate effect on GDP per se (e.g., damaged infrastructure, lost military systems, prompt and long-term care for casualties, seized assets), though any of these costs could be enormous.

Neither have we quantified a factor that could make China's losses substantially worse than those indicated below: the deepening integration of the East Asian economy. The economies of China and its neighbors (Japan, South Korea, Taiwan, and, increasingly, Southeast Asia) are highly interdependent, owing to production *value networks*. Much of East Asian trade is composed of intermediate goods and components: Inputs produced in one country are shipped to another country to be married with parts made elsewhere and assembled into a final product before being fed into market distribution systems. While such integration has contributed to the efficiency and productivity that have enabled China and its neighbors to prosper, it also heightens East Asian economies' vulnerability to disruption, more so than traditional end-

---

[17] Consummation of new East Asian or transpacific trade pacts will, if anything, deepen economic integration and trade expansion in the coming decade.

product trade would. China could reduce its dependence on such inter-locking regional production only with great difficulty and cost.

The primary effect on GDP is from loss of trade. We are most confident in the estimated collapse of Sino-U.S. bilateral trade, which empirically falls to virtually zero between belligerents in the course of war. But it is important also to take account of China's loss of regional and other global trade, given the war-zone effect. As shown in Figures 3.4 and 3.5, whether losses are confined to bilateral trade or may include all trade makes a big difference in China's GDP loss. Figure 3.4 shows the GDP impact from losses in trade, consumption, and income from investment, albeit with only bilateral Sino-U.S. trade affected. Figure 3.5 shows the GDP impact from losses in trade, consumption, and income from investment, with Chinese trade with the United

Figure 3.4
Estimated Aggregate Effect on GDP from Losses in *Bilateral* Trade, Consumption, and Income from Investment

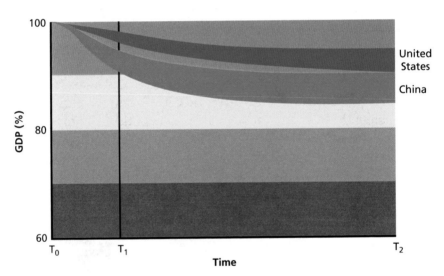

NOTES: This graph illustrates the percentage by which GDP may decrease during war as a result of losses in bilateral trade, consumption, and income from investment. The upper limit of the y-axis indicates GDP at the start of war; as the war continues, GDP at each point in time is given as a percentage of GDP at the start of war. The widths of the curves suggest uncertainty.
RAND RR1140-3.4

Figure 3.5
Estimated Aggregate Effect on GDP from Losses in *Overall* Trade, Consumption, and Income from Investment

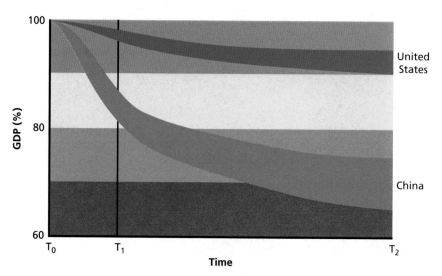

NOTES: This graph illustrates the percentage by which GDP may decrease during war as a result of losses in overall (bilateral, regional, and global) trade, consumption, and income from investment. The upper limit of the y-axis indicates GDP at the start of war; as the war continues, GDP at each point in time is given as a percentage of GDP at the start of war. The widths of the curves suggest uncertainty.
RAND *RR1140-3.5*

States, the region, and the rest of the world affected. The widths of the curves suggest uncertainty. As with military losses, T_2 is posited to be one year.

Now, consider what could happen to GDP if China's non-U.S. regional and global trade, nearly all of it seaborne, were also affected by widespread fighting in the Western Pacific. We assume that China's regional trade drops by 80 percent and its other global trade drops by 50 percent. (One reason regional and global trade do not drop even more is that Chinese shippers might be ordered by the state to continue operating.)

Indicative estimates of U.S. and Chinese economic costs of a prolonged severe war are summarized in Table 3.3, the analysis and sourcing for which can be found in Appendix B.

Table 3.3
Estimated Economic Costs After One Year of Severe War

Category	U.S. Costs	Chinese Costs
Trade	90 percent decline in bilateral trade	90 percent decline in bilateral trade 80 percent decline in regional trade 50 percent decline in global trade
Consumption	4 percent decline	4 percent decline
Income from foreign direct investment (asset loss excluded)	$9 billion loss	$500 million loss
Effects on GDP	Could decline by 5–10 percent	Could decline by 25–35 percent

The estimated decline in China's GDP can be compared with Germany's 29 percent decline in real GDP during World War I, when Germany itself was spared heavy damage, as well as Germany's 64 percent GDP decline and Japan's 52 percent GDP decline during World War II, when both were heavily attacked.[18] Of course, to suggest that the Chinese would be unwilling or unable to fight on despite such costs is to ignore that the Germans and Japanese withstood much greater costs, along with widespread destruction, and did not surrender until left with no choice. Moreover, the Chinese state would presumably work to limit the impact on consumption, as we have estimated. Still, the effects on China and its citizens of a one-third reduction in GDP would obviously be grave and lasting. In contrast, the effects of a protracted and severe conflict on the United States and its citizens, while severe, would also be the equivalent of a serious recession.

In a restricted and mild conflict, economic costs from lost trade, consumption, and income from overseas holdings would be similar in kind, substantially less in magnitude, and asymmetrically harmful to China.

In a more speculative vein, both China and the United States would be vulnerable to economic costs in the event that cyberwar,

---

[18] Robert J. Barro, "Rare Disasters and Asset Markets in the Twentieth Century," *Quarterly Journal of Economics*, Vol. 121, No. 3, August 2006.

which is likely to occur in a severe conflict, leapt from the military domain to civilian domains. While each nation would have a strong aversion to "general" cyberwar and so might be mutually deterred from attacking the other's nonmilitary computer networks, the ability to contain cyberwar, once begun, is unknown—if not unknowable.[19] Certain network infrastructure supports multiple computer systems, and certain computer systems that support military operations are also used for commercial or other civilian purposes. As an example, the supply of U.S. forces in a major armed conflict might depend on logistics firms, which rely mainly on open data systems, perhaps Internet-based, to manage and move material. Would China refrain from trying to degrade such systems in the event of war? Would the United States refrain from attacking, say, systems that support the transport of Chinese troops? Would both countries not be tempted to crash telecommunications or air-traffic control or energy-distribution systems that support fighting, or interfere with government-service networks? In short, the "firebreak" separating military-operational cyberwar from national-economic cyber could prove weak; once crossed, cyberwar could spin out of control, affecting all sorts of critical information infrastructure, the Internet, and commercial systems.

Very roughly speaking, China and the United States are equally vulnerable to the harm such civilian cyberwar could cause, because both economies and societies rely heavily on computer networks. Estimates of the economic damage from a series of large-scale cyberattacks on the United States range from $70 billion to $900 billion.[20] With at least 200 million more Internet users than the United States, China might have just as much to lose from targeting civilian cyber infrastructure as does the United States. China's economy has become very integrated internally and with the rest of the world, and that integration is enabled by potentially vulnerable data networking. Disrup-

---

[19] For analysis of the potential and possible paths of cyberwar escalation, see Lawrence Cavaiola, David Gompert, and Martin Libicki, "Cyber House Rules: On War, Retaliation and Escalation," *Survival: Global Politics and Strategy*, Vol. 57, No. 1, February–March 2015.

[20] Scott Borg, "How Cyber Attacks Will Be Used in International Conflict," paper presented at the USENIX Security Technology Symposium, Washington, D.C., 2010.

tion of both internal and external commerce resulting from cyberattacks could aggravate China's economic costs of war. Both countries are capable of patching, working around, and otherwise containing the effects of cyber attacks; however, the cumulative effects of multiple shocks in different sectors could cause appreciable reductions in production, commerce, and consumption. While we offer no estimate of the possible costs of escalating cyberwar, it is evident that they could be very large *on both sides* in the event of a severe and protracted Sino-U.S. conflict.

In sum, the economic harm caused by a Sino-U.S. war, unless brief or mild, would be substantially greater to China than to the United States, an asymmetry likely to persist if not grow by 2025. Unlike the military balance, there is little China can do, given its need for global markets and resources, to mitigate the economic risks of a war with the United States.[21] The economic integration that has made China's development possible exposes China to the risk that war could bring that development to a screeching halt. While this should darken any encouragement that China's military might feel or convey about a brightening military picture, it does not mean that the Chinese would be unwilling or unable to bear such a price. Losing great powers have endured much worse.

---

[21] Because China is currently a large net importer of food, the question arises whether its population is vulnerable to hunger in the event a war severely constricts seaborne trade. In fact, China keeps large grain reserves in the event of catastrophic events, such as crop failures or, in this case, war. In addition, in normal years, China remains domestically self-sufficient in rice and wheat, the most important staples in the Chinese diet. As a result, according to the World Bank, China's food self-sufficiency will remain above 90 percent through and beyond 2030. China could easily reduce consumption of meat and other agricultural products that depend on imported feeds and still provide sufficient food for all its citizens in the event of a conflict. See World Bank, *China Economic Update: Special Topic—Changing Food Consumption Patterns in China; Implications for Domestic Supply and International Trade*, Beijing, June 2014a, p. 26.

Political Effects

Domestic political responses effects of war would differ considerably between China and the United States because their political conditions are so different. We assume that those conditions would basically be the same in 2025 as in 2015. The nature, scale, and timing of political effects are, if anything, even harder to predict than military losses and economic costs. Whether those effects described below would occur during or after a conflict of one year (the period posited for a long war) is unknowable, but it is nonetheless worth considering.

China is a single-party authoritarian state with, at present, a powerful chief executive.[22] That leader is working to strengthen civilian control over the military.[23] Divisions among top civilian officials or between them and military chiefs or economic elites are slight or well masked. Public opinion, though an important source of pressure and potential cradle of dissent, is not critical to the regime's survival: The middle class is mainly patriotic in sentiment, the rural poor are voiceless, migrant factory workers are formless, and dissidents are a small minority and more concerned with political or religious freedom than foreign policy. Debate and protest are at the sufferance of the state. Access to information can be controlled, up to a point, given widespread Internet access. The state and its internal security apparatus have ample means to suppress opposition and the will to use those means. However, Beijing's commitment to domestic order reflects its fear of the sort of instability that China has experienced in the past and that could again engulf the country, threaten the regime, and leave China weak and vulnerable.

U.S. domestic politics are nearly the inverse of China's. At present, U.S. politics are polarized and the government is divided. Virtually any issue, even war and peace, can bring on criticism, partisan squab-

---

[22] See Elizabeth C. Economy, "China's Imperial President: Xi Jinping Tightens His Grip," *Foreign Affairs*, November–December 2014.

[23] There have been grounds for doubt that recent Chinese civilian leaders have as much control over the PLA as earlier leaders. However, Xi Jinping has taken steps to regain such control, without indications of PLA resistance.

bling, and partial paralysis.[24] The ability of the president to be an effective commander-in-chief could be impaired by politicization; opposition could come from peace factions, war factions, or both. Unless the country's security is directly threatened, the wholehearted support of the general public and the elite cannot be assumed, especially after costly wars with disappointing results in Iraq and Afghanistan. U.S. administrations persist in unpopular wars at their own peril. Neither patience nor continuity can be assumed, especially with elections every two years. At the same time, there is no doubt about the state's survival in the event of a war with huge losses and costs, as there might be in China's case.

Political responses, constraints, and consequences in the two countries could be strongly influenced by perceptions of the stakes of war. Matters concerning Chinese territorial claims, historical injustices, and sovereign rights would have strong purchase among Chinese elites and the public. Yet many Americans could regard such matters as peripheral to U.S. vital interests and not worth a costly war, unless unified leadership could convince them otherwise. As fighting lasts, these original interests could be altered by how the war is going in terms of casualties, economic impact, attacks on civilians, and popular anger or revulsion, making internal politics volatile and unpredictable.

The U.S. government could experience acute "tactical" political problems (e.g., partisan and popular polarization) throughout a conflict, whereas the Chinese government would have few such problems and the muscle to manage them. But China could face "strategic" political problems that the regime would have to confront in the event of a long and severe conflict. China's "rally round the flag" impulse could be stronger at first but then give way to instabilities that the United States does not face.

The president of the United States could be criticized from the outset for involving the country in a war over less-than-vital interests. Such criticism could be intensified by significant losses, especially

---

[24] As this is being written, the polarization along partisan lines that has dogged U.S. attempts to negotiate a nuclear-enrichment deal with Iran suggests erosion of the principle that politics end at the water's edge.

casualties, in severe fighting. On the other hand, the president could be criticized for timidity if he or she held back the U.S. military to limit hostilities and losses. Although civilian control of the military would not be in doubt, strains could appear over presidential micro-management, driven by concern with costs. While it is possible that mounting casualties could rally public support, especially if injected with anti-Chinese sentiment, it is also possible that opposition to war would grow. Depending on the stakes and reactions to losses, a long and severe war could divide the United States and aggravate problems of uncompromising partisanship and dysfunctional government.

While U.S. military advantages have until now offered the chance to win a war swiftly and so avoid such political pressures and pitfalls, this might be less likely in the future. The commander-in-chief could be in a vise between war-winning military logic and cost-containing political-economic logic. Whether its internal politics would permit the United States to fight a long, costly, and possibly inconclusive war with China would depend in part on the war's origin and the U.S. stake in its outcome. History suggests—and China should not overlook—that the United States is capable of considerable political stamina during war.

Political support, state control, and stability in both countries could also be subject to the effects of cyberwar, were it to escalate into civilian domains. Here, too, China could be more vulnerable insofar as the Chinese government relies more on influencing popular sentiment through media, the Internet, and other communications channels than does, or can, the U.S. government. If Beijing's ability to manipulate information, maintain support, and avert disorder is degraded, spontaneous and opposing opinions could roil segments of the population.

Expectations of how U.S. domestic politics would affect and be affected by war, depending on intensity and duration, are summarized in Table 3.4.

Strains on China's political system and cohesion would probably be manageable in the event of mild hostilities. Social networking could empower opposition to some extent, though the regime's ability to restrict and manipulate information and to contain dissent should prevail. A choice by the regime to limit hostilities to avoid major losses, attacks on China, and escalation could produce military grumbling

Table 3.4
Potential Effects on U.S. Domestic Politics in the Four Cases

		Brief	Long
Mild		Pressure from opponents of war could cause tight control over fighting (assuming China is also in that mode). But a brief and restricted conflict with an ambiguous outcome could lead to strong criticism from pro-war quarters.	Pro-war opponents could claim that politicians are tying the military's hands.
Severe		Pro-peace opposition could be too weak to prevent strong U.S. military action. However, pro-war support could constrain the U.S. ability to agree to terms for early cessation.	Mounting losses and economic damage could divide the country, impair prosecution of war, and make continuity of effort hostage to political change (e.g., elections).

but not outright defiance. Assuming that Chinese leaders and elites feel strongly about the conflict's stakes (e.g., matters of national sovereignty and honor), any opposition among the populace would not compel the regime to cease fighting.

However, severe hostilities, if prolonged, could generate domestic political turbulence and centrifugal forces. The danger of unrest derives from the dependence of the regime's legitimacy on economic well-being and patriotic pride; to the extent both are fractured by war losses and costs, segments of the society (e.g., elites, middle class, workers, and peasants) could sour on the leadership. Not just capital but also capitalists might flee the country. While domestic turmoil might not imperil the regime, it could force it to crack down on large swaths of an angry public, further undermining its legitimacy. The danger of separatism lies in the opportunity separatists in Tibet or Xinjiang might see if the state were preoccupied with a damaging and demanding war with the United States. Because significant PLA ground forces and other internal-security forces would presumably remain available even in the event of a major conflict with the United States, the regime would be able to crush separatists, but at a cost of resources and of domestic and international legitimacy at a time when both could be in short supply.

Expectations of how Chinese domestic politics would affect and be affected by war, depending on intensity and duration, are summarized in Table 3.5.

Juxtaposing possible U.S. and Chinese political effects, it seems that Chinese leaders would face little internal opposition in a brief conflict, regardless of its intensity, whereas U.S. leaders could face vehement opposition, partisanship, and polarization from the outset.[25] Moreover, Chinese leaders are able and willing to suppress domestic opposition. While patriotic support can be expected in both cases, it could be more fervent in China, especially if most Chinese feel more strongly than most Americans do about the national interests at stake in the conflict. However, in the event of a prolonged and costly conflict, China could

Table 3.5
Potential Effects on Chinese Domestic Politics in the Four Cases

	Brief	Long
Mild	Little elite or public opposition would arise. Separatists might see greater opportunity, but the regime's security apparatus could neutralize.	Elite, public, and perhaps military impatience could grow but not threaten the regime. Separatists might exploit conditions but not to the point of actually separating. The regime could increase oppression and lose some legitimacy, but not be in danger.
Severe	Elite and public support can be expected. However, Chinese heavy losses, poor prospects, and domestic turmoil might increase pressure to end the conflict, even on unfavorable terms, before instability flares. By 2025, the country might be unified in supporting war.	Mounting military losses and economic damage could weaken state legitimacy and increase dissent and unrest. Separatist activities could intensify and lead to greater repression. Internal strains could tax the state's resources and legitimacy at a time of costly war.

---

[25] Whether domestic political opposition impairs a U.S. administration's ability to wage war is mainly a function of the degree of congressional-executive disharmony, which might reflect public disharmony or opposition. It was not until well after a majority of Americans soured on the Vietnam War that Congress began implementing serious roadblocks against the U.S. war effort. The U.S. effort in Iraq, toward which the public became disenthralled, continued without effective congressional opposition. Having said this, a U.S. administration might be self-restrained if a war encounters major public opposition and exacts a major political cost.

face more-serious domestic upheaval than the United States would, which could motivate Beijing to seek peace.

International Effects

International effects of Sino-U.S. war can be thought of as concentric circles: general world opinion is outermost and least consequential; in the next circle, responses of major nonregional actors, including allies of either side; in the center and most important, East Asian states. Irrespective of their positions on the causes, merits, and favored side in a conflict, countries, institutions, and enterprises worldwide, fearful of economic harm, would appeal for an immediate end to Sino-U.S. combat. But such views are unlikely to sway either belligerent.

Of more significance than world opinion would be reactions of other powers, notably Russia, India, and European (NATO) states. India and Russia, China's most powerful land neighbors, are likely to be sympathetic to the United States and China, respectively. Although India would want to refrain from direct military intervention, it might increase readiness of its force along the frontier, especially if it felt its vital interests could be affected. This could cause China to do likewise with PLA ground forces (which would in any case not be heavily used against U.S. forces).

Russia is more of a wild card. While it lacks capabilities to conduct effective military operations in the Western Pacific, it could exploit U.S. preoccupation in the Pacific to increase threats to former Soviet states in Eastern Europe (e.g., Ukraine) and the Caucasus (e.g., Georgia), and even try to intimidate its Baltic neighbors despite their NATO membership. Another possibility—less likely but with very different significance—is that Russia could seize the opportunity of a Sino-U.S. war to strengthen its position in central Asia and Siberia at China's expense. Geopolitics aside, Russia would be eager to help China make up lost oil and gas supplies, though not for free. In addition, Russian arms could make up somewhat for Chinese military losses and expenditures (e.g., aircraft and air defense), though it would take time for them to be operationalized, and most would fare badly against U.S.

forces. Overall, though, Russia's economic weakness, military limitations, and dangers on or within its own frontiers reduce the importance of its support for China and the likelihood or significance of its intervention.

Assuming that its European allies see the United States as justified, they would likely back it politically, while urging that the conflict, end lest it escalate or ruin the world economy. Short of direct combat involvement, NATO itself might pledge support for U.S. efforts to oppose Chinese aggression. One of the most important European contributions would be to preempt or respond to any increased Russian pressure on Eastern Europe. In the course of a lengthy conflict, Europe might be willing to join in an embargo of export to China of any goods, technologies, and services that could aid its war effort.

As for other Chinese "allies," North Korea is even more unpredictable than Russia. Although North Korea no longer has the conventional military capability to invade and defeat South Korea, it could use missiles against South Korea or Japan; although Seoul would almost certainly not enter a war against China in any case, Tokyo's options would be complicated by North Korean belligerence.

A conflict between China and the United States could disturb the greater Middle East by providing an opening for heightened violence from Islamist-extremist and anti-Israel groups (ISIS, al Qaeda, Hamas, and Hezbollah). Middle East difficulties could place additional demands on U.S. naval and air forces at a moment when more of them are needed in the Western Pacific. Conversely, a shift of significant U.S. forces from U.S. Central Command to U.S. Pacific Command could add to the potential for instability in the Middle East. Increased violence, extremism, and instability in the Middle East could also be damaging to China, which gets much of its oil from there (though most oil would not ship through the war zone anyway).

East Asian states would have the most to lose from a Sino-U.S. war: Much of the region could be a war zone; its trade-intensive economy could go into depression; China might emerge either dominant or unstable; the region's extraordinary gains in security and prosperity could be threatened. Most East Asian states would want to see war end swiftly in military victory for the United States, but with China intact.

Most of China's neighbors have edged toward closer security relations with the United States. This drift could be accentuated in a conflict perceived to result from Chinese bellicosity.

The most critical state is Japan, with its growing military strength, its antagonistic relationship with China, and the strong possibility that China would attack U.S. air bases on Japanese territory. Recent reinterpretation of Japan's constitution, at the initiative of the Abe government, effectively legalizes military support for the United States in a war with China.[26] Of course, the probability of significant Japanese involvement in the war would be greater if Japan was involved in the issue or confrontation that triggered conflict (e.g., in the East China Sea). Japanese military participation would be virtually assured if China were to attack Japan, including U.S. bases in Japan, or Japanese forces. While China has the option of not attacking U.S. bases on Japanese territory, such a decision would involve major operational drawbacks.

As for capabilities, Japanese submarines, surface combatants, combat aircraft, strike weapons, and ISR could make a material difference in a severe war by 2025. The longer a Sino-U.S. conflict lasted, the greater the potential effect of Japanese military contributions on the U.S. side. In a long, severe war, China would find it difficult to contend with combined U.S. and Japanese forces, as the latter made up for the former's attrition. Moreover, Japanese involvement would reduce the need for the United States to strip its forces from elsewhere for reinforcement.

Overall, Japanese combat involvement could increase Chinese losses and offset or even reduce U.S. losses in a long, severe conflict. Because Japan's forces are being steadily improved, its entry could widen the gap between U.S. and Chinese losses in 2025 that was depicted above. This possibility reinforces the observation already made that even with improved Chinese A2AD and reduced U.S. military superi-

---

[26] This assumes adequate domestic political support for Japanese intervention. Notwithstanding the reinterpretation of the constitution, polls suggest that a majority of Japanese continue to oppose involvement in wars other than in self-defense. See, e.g., Kamiya Matake, "Japanese Public Opinions About the Exercise of the Right of Collective Self-Defense," *Discuss Japan*, September 25, 2014.

ority, China cannot be confident of winning a long, severe war. At the same time, Japanese intervention would enrage the Chinese and could enflame, extend, or expand the conflict. It might cause China to fight longer and endure greater costs than it would otherwise. China might widen attacks on Japan, though at the price of diverting forces already under heavy attack and stress.

Depending on the cause and locus of the conflict, other East Asian states would mostly side with the United States in varying degrees: from support ranging from permission to use bases to the possible commitment of forces (e.g., Australia, New Zealand, the Philippines), to cautious support for the United States among countries with strong ties to China (notably, South Korea) or significant Chinese populations (e.g., Singapore, Malaysia, Indonesia, Thailand), to support for China (only North Korea). The participation of Australian forces, because of their quality, could have military significance despite their small size. Apart from military contributions, the longer and more severe the conflict, the more and perhaps more permanently China could become isolated from the very region it aspires to lead. This, in turn, could strengthen pro-peace voices in Beijing (e.g., in the Ministry of Foreign Affairs).[27]

Prognostications about the reaction of third parties are fraught with uncertainty even now, let alone ten years from now. Much would depend on the cause of war: For example, a Chinese move to gain control of the East or South China Seas flagrant enough to force U.S. armed intervention would be more likely to produce a significant anti-China international response than would a conflict over Taiwan, especially if it appeared that the Chinese were provoked. It is conceivable that many U.S. friends, near and far, would lay low or that Russia or North Korea would act in ways that added to U.S. military risks and burdens. Yet another possibility, touched on in the earlier discussion of "upper limits" of war, is that many states would be dragged in or enter

---

[27] In terms of sheer mass, the combined GDP (approximately $10 trillion) of Asian states that would favor the United States is roughly equivalent to China's, and the combined defense spending of those states (approximately $150 billion) is nearly as great as China's (Stockholm International Peace Research Institute, *SIPRI Yearbook 2014: Armaments, Disarmament and International Security*, Oxford, UK: Oxford University Press, 2014).

opportunistically, leading to a quasi–world war. However, we think the more likely international reaction would be for regional states with direct and critical interests, such as Japan, to get involved, mainly to the disadvantage of China.

In sum, world public opinion would favor the immediate cessation of fighting. Russia might growl, posture, and exploit a Sino-U.S. conflict by taking initiatives elsewhere, whether or not in sync with China. Some East Asian states, in varying degrees, would line up behind the United States. Japan's involvement could make a long, severe conflict more costly for China but could also increase the dangers of escalation.

These international effects would be amplified, to the advantage of the United States, the longer a severe war persisted. Possible international responses are summarized in Table 3.6.

The Four Cases and Their Effects

Each category of effects is important in its own right and in its implications for other effects:

- Military losses can affect the ability, especially of China, to keep trade going, prevent destruction of infrastructure, and maintain access to energy supplies.

Table 3.6
Possible International Responses in the Four Cases

	Brief	**Long**
Mild	Regional and global pressure on both sides to end conflict.	NATO support would enable the United States to concentrate more forces in the Western Pacific.
Severe	International shock and pressure on both sides to end conflict. Warnings and military preparations by Japan and other East Asian states. Russia provides indirect support for China, as NATO does for United States.	Japanese and other East Asian entry in support of the United States. India could exploit the frontier to the disadvantage of China. NATO could limit exploitation by Russia.

- New domains of warfare—cyberspace and space—can have both a military and economic effect, given that dual-use systems (e.g., communications, logistics networks, GPS) could be disabled.
- Cyberwar, if not confined to military networks, could hinder political responses to war, affect third parties, and compound economic disruptions.
- Economic costs, whether from hostilities or from disruption of commerce, would affect the ability of combatants to make up for military losses in a severe and protracted conflict.
- Economic hardship, such as reduced consumption of and access to essentials, could affect political support, stability, and cohesion, and thus the ability and resolve of each side to continue fighting at a high intensity.
- Adverse world public opinion directed at one or both parties would make little difference in their ability and will to fight, at least in the short term. However, the reactions of important third parties could eventually help one side or the other in major ways: direct combat, war supplies, trade, energy access, and, in the case of the United States, support in other theaters that enables concentration of forces.

Table 3.7 *integrates* the four categories of effects on both states in the four conflict cases. (The "Military" column includes 2015 and 2025 cases to reflect the effects of improvements in Chinese A2AD.) The "General" column and row summarize the four cases and the four sorts of effects, respectively, providing a very rough sense of the impact on and relative advantage of the sides.

Overall, the decline in U.S. warfighting advantages does not mean China can win a war that the United States is willing to fight. By 2025, a war could be a military standoff, with major weapon-platform losses on both sides, in addition to losses in cyberspace and space. Yet neither side would fare so much worse than the other that it would feel compelled to concede, raising the probability that a war would be both severe and long. Such a war could be decided by economic costs, domestic political effects, and international responses. Japan's

Table 3.7
Possible Effects on the United States and China in the Four Cases and Overall

	Military	Economic	Political	International	General
Brief, mild	Minor losses on both sides.	China: Broad but brief disruption of trade, consumption, and energy. United States: Brief disruption of trade with China.	China: Little elite or public opposition. The PLA favors intensified attacks but does not openly challenge the regime. Separatists see greater opportunity, but the regime and its internal security apparatus neutralize it. United States: Pressure from both sides: doves demanding cessation, and hawks demanding stepped-up strikes.	Regional and global pressure on both sides to end conflict.	Brief but serious economic disruption, asymmetrically harming China.
Brief, severe	2015 China: U.S. counterforce capabilities take a major toll early and throughout. United States: Chinese A2AD takes a major early toll but then less as degraded by U.S. strikes. 2025 China: Increased U.S. losses reduce strike threat to Chinese forces. United States: Improved and less vulnerable Chinese A2AD produces increased U.S. losses.	China: Shock to global trade, with aftershocks to consumption, energy supply. Difficult recovery. United States: Brief economic disruption, confined to trade with and investment in China. Quick recovery.	China: Elite and public supportive. The PLA is satisfied. Early support is stronger in 2025 with better military results. United States: Doves too weak to prevent strong U.S. military action. Hawks constrain U.S. ability to agree to terms for early cessation.	Regional and global shock. Pressure on both sides to end conflict. Warnings and military preparations by Japan and other East Asian states. Russia voices support for China and NATO for the United States.	Major military losses and economic costs for both, but asymmetrically harming China. Gap in expected losses less unfavorable to China in 2025 than in 2015.

Table 3.7—Continued

	Military	Economic	Political	International	General
Long, mild	Modest losses of aircraft or ships on both sides.	**China:** Serious compounding damage to trade, consumption, and energy supply. Slow and difficult recovery. **United States:** Significant economic harm from disrupted trade with and investment in China. Slow recovery.	**China:** Elite, public, and PLA impatience grow but do not threaten the regime. Separatists try to exploit conditions. The regime becomes more oppressive and less legitimate, but not in danger. **United States:** Hawks claim that politicians are tying the military's hands.	NATO support elsewhere enables the United States to concentrate more forces in Western Pacific.	Economic costs more harmful to China. Domestic dissatisfaction grows in both states. International responses favor the United States.
Long, severe	**2015** **China:** U.S. strike capabilities, though somewhat degraded by A2AD, take a major toll on Chinese forces. Extensive damage to war-related infrastructure. Computer and satellite degradation. **United States:** Chinese A2AD takes a major toll on U.S. forces early but less as degraded by U.S. strikes. **2025** **China:** Improved A2AD reduces losses somewhat, though still greater than U.S. losses. Increased cyber and satellite losses. **United States:** Improved and less vulnerable Chinese A2AD produces increased U.S. losses early and throughout. Increased cyber and satellite losses.	U.S. GDP falls by 5–10 percent in one year. China's GDP falls by 25–35 percent in one year. Escalating cyberwar aggravates turmoil in both economies.	**China:** Mounting military losses and economic damage weaken state legitimacy and increase dissent and unrest. Separatist activities intensify and lead to greater repression. While internal strains do not imperil the state, they tax it severely at a time of costly war. **United States:** Mounting losses and economic costs divide the country, impair prosecution of war, and make continuity of effort hostage to political change.	Japanese and other East Asian countries enter in support of the United States. China is concerned that India could exploit the situation on the frontier. NATO limits Russia exploitation.	Major losses. Reduction in the military capabilities of both sides. Asymmetrically severe economic costs (including cyber and space), for China. Possible Chinese domestic instability. International response favors the United States.

Table 3.7—Continued

	Military	Economic	Political	International	General
General	As U.S. military advantages decline by 2025, U.S. losses increase, Chinese losses decrease, and the prospect of outright U.S. military victory declines. Growing cyber and satellite losses on both sides.	China is far more vulnerable than the United States to broad, deep, and lasting economic harm.	China is better equipped than the United States to contain the political effects of a short war, but China faces challenges in a long one.	U.S. East Asian allies provide significant support in a persisting conflict. Japan's entry has a significant military effect by 2025. NATO allies and India are be indirectly helpful to the United States, as Russia is to China.	

entry could offset the decline of U.S. military superiority, especially in a prolonged conflict. All these factors, taken together, would strongly favor the United States.

Recall the earlier observation that war between China and the United States could be worse than the long, severe case, as described here. In the 20th century, two great-power wars became world wars, and a third could have followed the same course, or even worse. The possibility of a Sino-U.S. war drawing in other powers and many states cannot be excluded: In addition to Japan, perhaps India, Vietnam, and NATO would be on the U.S. side; Russia and North Korea would be on China's side. Fighting could spread beyond the region. War aims could expand, and as they did, so would the costs of losing. Even if nuclear weapons were not used, China might find other ways to attack the United States proper. Use of space and cyberspace could be severely curtailed. As long as fighting remained inclusive, destruction and hardship could fuel determination and further mobilization. In sum, both the duration and severity of war could exceed the upper case used here for purposes of analysis. If so, losses and costs would be even greater for both sides and the world, and the outcome would be no more favorable for China, despite the expansion of its power.

CHAPTER FOUR

Findings, Recommendations, and Concluding Observations

Findings

Unless both U.S. and Chinese political leaders decline to authorize their militaries to carry out their counterforce strategies, the ability of either state to control the ensuing conflict would be greatly impaired. Both would suffer large military losses from the outset and throughout a severe conflict: In 2015, U.S. losses could be a relatively small fraction of forces committed, but still significant; Chinese losses could be much heavier than U.S. losses and a substantial fraction of forces committed. This gap in losses will shrink as Chinese A2AD improves: By 2025, U.S. losses could range from significant to heavy; Chinese losses, while still very heavy, could be somewhat less than in 2015, owing to increased degradation of U.S. strike capabilities. A severe and lengthy conflict would leave both with substantially reduced total military capacity and thus vulnerable to other threats.

China's A2AD will make it increasingly difficult for the United States to gain military-operational dominance and victory, even in a long war. However, provided the United States is nonetheless willing to fight, China cannot expect to win militarily. Thus, the two could face the prospect of an extremely costly military standoff.

This outcome implies that a conflict could be decided by domestic political, international, and, especially, economic factors, all of which would favor the United States in a long, severe war:

- Although a war would harm both economies, damage to China's would be far worse (perhaps 25–35 percent of GDP after one year). Because much of the Western Pacific would become a war zone, China's trade with the region and the rest of the world would decline substantially. China's loss of seaborne energy supplies would be especially damaging. Although consumption is a smaller share of the Chinese economy than the U.S. economy, it is expected to grow, leaving the Chinese economy vulnerable to further contraction in the event of war.

- Politically, a long conflict, especially if militarily severe and economically punishing, could expose China to internal division—taxing and testing the state.
- The entry of Japan and, to a lesser extent, other U.S. partners in the region could have a considerable influence on military operations. The responses of Russia, India, and NATO are less important. However, NATO efforts to preserve security in other regions (at least Europe, if not also the Middle East) would permit greater, or less risky, commitment of U.S. forces to war with China. Such a combination of international responses could increase Chinese losses in a long, severe conflict, despite improved A2AD.

In a nutshell, despite military trends that favor it, China could not win, and might lose, a severe war with the United States in 2025, especially if prolonged. Moreover, the economic costs and political dangers of such a war could imperil China's stability, end its development, and undermine the legitimacy of the state.

Yet in the event of war, the military capabilities, motivations, and plans of both sides make a severe, prolonged, and exceedingly costly conflict a distinct possibility. Of the many reasons the United States should not want such a war, the most important are the immense military losses and economic costs to itself and the implications, for the country, the region, and the world, of devastating harm to China. Such prospects underscore the importance of both the United States and China contemplating how to control and restrict fighting should a crisis turn violent, which shines the spotlight on principles and procedures for political control and communication.

Recommendations

The findings confirm what is widely thought: A Sino-U.S. war would be so harmful that both sides should place a very high priority on avoiding one. While such prospects make premeditated war highly improbable, they also dictate effective individual and bilateral crisis management, as well as other measures to avoid misperceptions and mistakes.

Because the United States might be unable to control, win, or avoid major losses and costs of a severe conflict, it must guard against automaticity in implementing immediate attacks on Chinese A2AD and should have plans and means to prevent hostilities from becoming severe. Establishing "fail safe" arrangements will guarantee definitive, informed political approval for military operations.

Likewise, China has much to lose from a severe conflict, and even more from a prolonged, severe one. Notwithstanding favorable military trends, China has as much reason as the United States to avoid automatic execution of military plans for a sharp and immediate counterforce exchange, including a parallel requirement for unambiguous political control. Again, if *either* state executes its military plans to strike the forces of the other, a severe war would likely ensue.

Thus, it is necessary but not sufficient for the United States to be able to refrain from full execution of military plans once fighting begins, for it could not hesitate to strike hard if China does or is about to do so. Given the extreme penalty for allowing one's forces to be struck before they strike, creating mutual forbearance at the outset of hostilities could be as difficult as it is critical. It requires an ability to cooperate at a moment of intense pressure to attack, which in turn makes clear, direct, and prompt political communication as important after as it is before hostilities begin. *Together with ensuring that U.S. and Chinese political leaders alike have military options other than immediate strikes to destroy opposing forces, having the means to confer and contain a conflict before it gets out of hand is the most important recommendation coming out of this analysis.*

Along with measures to prevent crises from becoming violent and violence from becoming severe, the United States should try to reduce the effect of Chinese A2AD in the coming years. Work at RAND and elsewhere increasingly stresses the need to invest in more-survivable force platforms (e.g., submarines) and in counter-A2AD (e.g., theater missiles). Such efforts would buttress deterrence, help prevent increased China's confidence of prevailing in a severe conflict, and improve stability in crises, as well as in the critical initial stage of a conflict. But the efforts would not dramatically reduce U.S. military losses or economic costs of a severe conflict.

Even as China's military capabilities improve, it would suffer huge losses in a long, severe conflict. Moreover, the economic, domestic, and international effects of a long, severe conflict work against China. The United States needs to be sure that the Chinese are specifically aware of the potential for catastrophic results even if a war is not lost militarily.

While not losing sight of the grave harm to the United States of a lengthy and severe conflict, prudent U.S. preparations for one would help disabuse the Chinese of expecting victory at acceptable cost. However, a heavy dose of common sense is needed in contemplating such preparations. As stressed from the outset of this study, war with China is improbable, in part because both sides know that the costs would outweigh the gains, even for the winner—if indeed there is one. Moreover, the costs of being completely prepared are prohibitive—undoubtedly greater than the costs of war when discounted by the low probability of one.

With this in mind, U.S. preparations fall into several categories:

- Improving the ability to sustain severely intense military operations: The Department of Defense should analyze critical "consumables" (weapons and provisions) that could run out and tip the balance in the event a protracted war.
- Shifting toward more-survivable platforms: The Pentagon should not increase stocks of vulnerable platforms (surface ships and manned aircraft) that are expected to take significant losses, because of China's A2AD. Rather, the Pentagon should undertake a purposeful long-term program to substitute more-survivable systems, at least for this region.
- Improving U.S. and allied warfighting capabilities: In addition to improve survivability, U.S. and allied forces should exploit

more strategically the technologies that China is exploiting in its A2AD, including targeting, theater-range missiles, advanced extend-range air defense, and submarines.

- Conducting contingency planning with key allies: Japan is the most important but also the most controversial ally; however, existing low-profile U.S.-Japanese military planning is an established framework (well known to the Chinese) that could begin to touch on issues regarding low-probability and high-consequence conflict with China. Similar planning with other East Asia allies is encouraged. NATO planning should be stretched in the direction of how European allies would respond to a Russian threat if the United States were in a major war with China. Again, this is a delicate matter and best done with no fanfare.

- Undertaking measures to mitigate the interruption of critical products from China: Here again, sound judgment must prevail. For the United States to slash Chinese imports in the off chance of a war would be to harm its own economy in anticipation of an unlikely event, which, though economically painful, would not be catastrophic. It would suffice for the United States government to identify alternative domestic and foreign sources of only the most critical products and parts made in China. This could include stockpiling especially vital materials.

- Developing options to deny China access to war-critical commodities and technologies in the event of war: Although a general U.S. blockade would not be needed to harm the Chinese economy, the United States could take measures that would make it difficult for China to sustain long and severe combat. Cutting off Chinese access to seaborne supplies of oil and liquefied natural gas would have the most dramatic effect. Although Russia would probably be eager and able to supply China with military hardware during a war, Chinese access to more-sophisticated Western systems could be stopped.

Such U.S. measures could reinforce Chinese perceptions that the United States is determined to encircle and isolate China, as well as create perceptions that the United States would seek to devastate China and destroy its state in the event of war. The distinction worth making is that the United States does not seek to isolate China unless war requires it to do so. The risk of harm to Sino-U.S. relations can be mitigated, though to only some extent, by patient and persistent efforts by the United States to engage Chinese political and military counterparts in discussion of cooperation and crisis management.

The U.S. Army, as a Title X service and in its joint responsibilities, has important roles to play in many aspects of such preparations. It should do the following:

- Invest in land-based A2AD capabilities (e.g., mobile theater-range missiles and advanced air defenses) to contribute to high Chinese military losses.
- Encourage and enable East Asian partners to mount strong defense, including missiles and air defense.
- Improve interoperability with partners, especially Japan.
- Contribute to the expansion and deepening of Sino-U.S. military-to-military understanding and cooperation to reduce dangers of misperception and miscalculation.

Because a Sino-U.S. war, in the construct used here, would not include a major ground combat, the U.S. Army's expected losses would be proportionately less than those of the Navy and Air Force. Therefore, this analysis does not change current planning factors concerning overall end-strength or mobilization requirements—albeit with important investments in technology and platforms and shifts in force structure to enhance long-range fires and air defense, as noted. However, a major conflict on the Korean peninsula would alter this presumption.

Concluding Observations

As China's military improvements neutralize the military advantages of the United States, and because technology favors conventional counterforce, war between the two countries could be intense, last a year or more, have no winner, and inflict huge losses and costs on both sides. The longer such a war continued, the more significant economic, domestic political, and international effects would become. While such nonmilitary effects would hit China hardest, they could also greatly harm the U.S. economy and the U.S. ability to meet security challenges worldwide. The United States should make prudent preparations to be able to wage a long and intense war with China. Of no less importance is the ability of the United States to limit the scope, intensity, and duration of a war with China through its planning, its system of civilian control, and its ability to communicate with China in peace, crisis, and war.

Likewise for China, political control and good wartime top-level communications are imperative. True, Chinese military improvements have lessened the danger of losing decisively to the United States. Yet China cannot count on a short war, and a long one could leave China weak, unstable, insecure, and impoverished.

To paraphrase Frederick the Great, evenly matched well-armed powers considering war will want to weigh whether possible gains would even "pay the interest" on probable costs. As the United States and China become more equal in their ability to destroy each other's forces, neither can be confident of winning at an acceptable price. Should a confrontation or incident nonetheless lead to hostilities, it would be better if both sides had thought through how to limit the harm, not just how to win.

Military Losses

Mild Case

Brief, Mild

- The conflict trigger event results in immediate losses for both sides.
- China suffers slightly more losses as a result of its lower levels of modern combat experience and less capable systems and platforms.

Long, Mild

- Protracted hostilities result in additional but relatively infrequent losses over the length of the conflict.
- China suffers slightly more losses because of less modern combat experience and less capable systems and platforms.

Severe Case, 2015

Table A.1 displays the expected military losses in the severe case for 2015.

Table A.1
Military Losses in the Severe Case, 2015

System Type	U.S. T_1	U.S. T_2	China T_1	China T_2
Aircraft				
Surface ships				
Submarines				
Missiles				
C4ISR				

NOTES: Green signifies modest losses; yellow, significant losses; orange, heavy losses; and red, very heavy losses. A mix of two colors in one cell indicates a range (e.g., green/yellow means we expect there would be modest to significant losses). T_1 = a hypothetical moment, within days of the start of the conflict, when the sides decide whether to continue fighting; T_2 = one year.

Aircraft
U.S. Losses

- No specific judgment is made here about whether China would damage or sink a U.S. aircraft carrier with an accompanying air wing.
- The United States would likely lose substantial forces initially in the region because of Chinese missile forces more so than Chinese aircraft. China has relatively few modern aircraft, and the newest generation would not yet be deployed.
- U.S. regional air bases would also come under attack, but China has limited aerial refueling to sustain operations against regional bases.
- The United States would have the edge in air-to-air combat.
- U.S. aircraft carriers would be vulnerable to Chinese submarines.

China's Losses

- Once China's most modern aircraft are incapacitated, China would be heavily dependent on outdated and aging airframes that have limited data relay capabilities. This means that Chinese aircraft would become increasingly vulnerable to U.S. aircraft during a conflict.

- However, China has a lot of places to hide aircraft, such as inland bases and tunnel facilities, and might choose to do so rather than have them shot down.
- China also has no modern experience sustaining air operations over long periods of time and has limited aerial refueling capabilities, which would affect sortie rates.

Surface Ships
U.S. Losses

- No specific judgment is made here about whether China would damage or sink a U.S. aircraft carrier with an accompanying air wing.
- The United States is likely to lose substantial forces initially in the region because of missile forces and, possibly, swarming techniques by PLA Navy (PLAN) and nonmilitary ships.
- Regional naval bases would also be under attack.
- U.S. ships could hide out far from the conflict in the deep Pacific.

China's Losses

- Chinese ships would be vulnerable to attack by U.S. submarines, particularly given Chinese weakness in ASW, as well as U.S. surface ships, planes, and so on.
- Chinese naval bases would be vulnerable as well, given that all are relatively near the potential theater of conflict, and Chinese ships would have nowhere to hide where they could also resupply.
- Although China has huge numbers of shipbuilding facilities and would likely be able to ramp up production as losses accumulated, no new ships would come online in time to affect the conflict.

Submarines
U.S. Losses

- U.S. submarines are relatively quiet and difficult for China to find.
- China has noted weaknesses in conducting ASW.
- U.S. submarine-launched missiles have a longer range than Chinese submarine-launched missiles, so the United States could participate farther from the fight.

China's Losses

- Even the newest Chinese submarines are still relatively noisy and easy to find. They would survive "well" (only in a comparative sense), but after they were incapacitated, the older, noisier ones would be easier to hunt down and destroy.
- The depletion of the Chinese submarine capability would make the U.S. submarine force even more survivable.

Missiles
U.S. Losses and Use of Missile Inventories

- The United States has large quantities of a variety of missiles, as well as a relatively diverse set of platforms from which to launch them.
- Some U.S. missile launchers (e.g., surface ships) are increasingly vulnerable. Air-to-surface missiles are only as survivable as the platforms that carry them.
- U.S. land-based missiles between 500 km and 5,500 km are prohibited by the Intermediate-Range Nuclear Forces (INF) treaty, whereas the Chinese missiles are not, giving China a significant advantage.
- Chinese long-range multiple launch rocket systems (MLRSs) have ranges that approximate those of U.S. land-based missiles. U.S. MLRSs do not have ranges that would make them useful.

China's Losses and Use of Missile Inventories

- China would use many missiles in initial waves and would eventually have to rely on older missiles with shorter ranges and more-limited capability.
- However, launchers would be relatively survivable given Second Artillery's extensive tunneling system.
- China might also hide some launchers to prevent the United States from targeting them and later deploy them in short bursts.

C4ISR

Both countries have some cyberwar and ASAT capabilities. However, China's capabilities are less tested and rugged and would likely wear down faster.

U.S. Losses

- China would be able to disable some U.S. satellites and broader C4ISR capabilities.
- However, the U.S. C4ISR capability is more robust and redundant than China's, so the United States would suffer lower degradation of capability after it survived the first wave.

China's Losses

- China depends less on C4ISR than the United States, but China would also have a much less robust capability once initial C4ISR capabilities were knocked out.
- The United States would focus attacks on Chinese sensors.
- The United States would also be able to knock out a lot of Chinese satellites in initial waves, and China would be hard-pressed to defend its remaining satellites.
- On the organizational side, China already suffers from command issues because of its stultified military organizational structure

and hierarchical command authority, both of which would likely exacerbate problems in wartime.[1]

Severe Case, 2025

Table A.2 displays the expected military losses in the severe case for 2025.

Aircraft
U.S. Losses

- Fifth-generation Chinese aircraft would be coming online and would represent a bigger threat to the United States, along with larger Chinese missile inventories.

Table A.2
Military Losses in the Severe Case, 2025

System Type	U.S. T_1	U.S. T_2	China T_1	China T_2
Aircraft				
Surface ships				
Submarines				
Missiles				
C4ISR				

NOTES: Green signifies modest losses; yellow, significant losses; orange, heavy losses; and red, very heavy losses. A mix of two colors in one cell indicates a range (e.g., green/yellow means we expect there would be modest to significant losses). T_1 = a hypothetical moment, within days of the start of the conflict, when the sides decide whether to continue fighting; T_2 = one year. In the categories where the assessments appear similar for both countries (aircraft for both T_1 and T_2 and C4ISR for T_1), we assess that Chinese attrition would be relatively greater than that of committed U.S. forces.

---

[1] For more information on organizational weaknesses within the PLA, see Michael S. Chase, Jeffrey G. Engstrom, Tai Ming Cheung, Kristen Gunness, Scott Warren Harold, Susan Puska, and Samuel K. Berkowitz, *China's Incomplete Military Transformation: Assessing the Weaknesses of the People's Liberation Army (PLA)*, Santa Monica, Calif.: RAND Corporation, RR-893-USCC, 2015.

- China would be more likely to damage or sink a U.S. aircraft carrier (or multiple carriers) and any accompanying air wings.
- The United States would likely lose a lot of forces initially in region, though still as a result of missile forces more so than Chinese aircraft.
- U.S. regional air bases would come under attack given that China would have a robust aerial refueling capability.
- The United States is still likely to have a qualitative edge in air-to-air combat but would have to fight a larger number of relatively new Chinese planes.
- U.S. fourth-generation aircraft would be in significant danger from Chinese fifth-generation aircraft.

China's Losses

- U.S. next-generation aircraft would be online.
- Newer Chinese planes would be equipped with data links and networked, improving information sharing and likely reducing losses.
- Depending on production rates of new aircraft, China would likely have a deeper bench of new aircraft than in 2015 and would therefore depend less on outdated and aging airframes.
- China would likely still lack modern experience sustaining air operations over long periods of time.
- However, China would also still have many places to hide aircraft, such as inland bases and tunnel facilities, and might choose to do so rather than have them shot down; or China might rotate them in and out of well-defended interior areas. By 2025, China would have two to three aircraft carriers and accompanying air wings that could be disabled or destroyed.

Surface Ships
U.S. Losses

- China is more likely to damage or sink a U.S. aircraft carrier (or multiple carriers).
- The United States is likely to lose substantial forces initially in region as a result of attacks by Chinese aircraft, missile forces, and, possibly, swarming techniques by PLAN and nonmilitary ships.
- U.S. regional naval bases would also be attacked.

China's Losses

- The United States is still likely to sink Chinese aircraft carriers.
- China has likely dealt with at least some ASW weaknesses, so Chinese surface ships would be less vulnerable to U.S. submarines.
- Chinese naval bases would still be vulnerable, given that all are relatively near the potential conflict theater, but ships might be able to resupply at foreign ports.
- However, the United States might be able to knock out Chinese ships in third-party locations, given its superior global military posture.
- China would be even better equipped to ramp up shipbuilding production, but few new ships would come online in time to affect a conflict.

Submarines
U.S. Losses

- U.S. submarines are quiet and difficult for China to target, despite improved ASW.

China's Losses

- The newest Chinese submarine classes would be much quieter, but there would be only a few of each class, and older submarines would still be detectable.
- Missile ranges on the new submarine-class missile will be longer, so these submarines will be able to participate in a conflict farther from the fight. The newest Chinese submarines would survive well, but the older ones would still be easy to hunt down and incapacitate.

Missiles
U.S. Losses and Use of Missile Inventories

- The United States would still have large quantities of a variety of different missiles, as well as a relatively more diverse set of platforms from which to launch missiles, with the exception of land-based missiles.
- However, the United States would face more-severe initial and protracted losses as a result of attacks on regional U.S. bases.
- The United States would not be able to bring enough tactical strike power or ISR to find and take down Chinese launchers, and U.S. survivability would be a problem.
- U.S. land-based missiles from 500 km to 5,500 km are prohibited by the INF treaty, whereas the Chinese missiles are not, giving China a significant advantage.
- Chinese long-range MLRSs have ranges that approximate those of U.S. land-based missiles. U.S. MLRSs do not have ranges that would make them useful.

China's Losses and Use of Missile Inventories

- China would have significantly more missiles and launchers in 2025.

- China's missile inventories would last longer, but China would still eventually have to rely on older missiles with shorter ranges and more-limited capability. Chinese launchers would be even more survivable and difficult to disable when hiding in the tunnels but would still largely be viable targets during above-ground launches.

C4ISR

Compared with 2015, C4ISR losses in 2025 could be worse for both sides, because both could take down C4ISR with systems that are relatively invulnerable.

U.S. Losses

- The United States would lose a lot more general C4ISR capability initially than in the 2015 scenario. China would also likely be better in 2025 than in 2015 at incapacitating U.S. satellites, and with improved sensing and long-range fires, China could do significant damage to ground components of the C4ISR networks.
- After the initial onslaught, China would have more-robust surviving capability to continue attacking U.S. C4ISR than in 2015, so the degradation of U.S. capabilities would continue.

China's Losses

- China would still depend less than the United States on C4ISR, but China's capability would also be more robust and networked than in 2015, so C4ISR losses would affect Chinese combat capability more. China is also likely to have many more satellites in 2025.
- Some reforms would likely have been made to the PLA's organizational structure and hierarchical command authority, but weaknesses in these areas would likely continue, especially if the PLA has not gained any recent combat experience.

Economic Effects in the Severe Case, 2015

Trade

- Glick and Taylor found that, on average, there is an 80 percent immediate drop in trade between adversaries when war commences.[1]
- There was a 96 percent drop in trade in World War I and a 97 percent decline in trade in World War II; trade between adversaries in these wars was "almost totally destroyed."[2]
- Therefore, we assume a 90 percent drop in bilateral trade (between the United States and China) after one year of severe conflict.
- Every 1 percent increase in trade, divided by GDP, equals a 1.97 percent increase in GDP per capita.[3]

U.S. Losses

- Total bilateral trade in 2013 equaled $562 billion.
- U.S. GDP in 2014 equaled $17.4 trillion.
- For the United States, a 90 percent loss in bilateral trade equals a 3 percent decrease in trade, divided by GDP, which leads to a

---

[1] Reuven Glick and Alan M. Taylor, "Collateral Damage: Trade Disruption and the Economic Impact of War," *Review of Economics and Statistics*, Vol. 92, No. 1, February 2010, p. 108.

[2] Glick and Taylor, 2010, p. 109.

[3] Jeffrey A. Frankel and David Romer, "Does Trade Cause Growth?" *American Economic Review*, Vol. 89, No. 3, June 1999, p. 385.

6 percent decrease in GDP per capita (per year). (See Figures B.1 and B.2.)

- The United States would suffer a 6 percent decrease in GDP after one year as a result of a 90 percent bilateral trade loss.

China's Losses

- Total bilateral trade in 2013 equaled $562 billion.
- China's GDP in 2014 equaled $9.2 trillion.
- For China, a 90 percent loss in bilateral trade equals a 5 percent decrease in trade, divided by GDP, which leads to a 10 percent decrease in GDP per capita (per year). (See Figures B.1 and B.2.)
- China would suffer a 10 percent decrease in GDP after one year as a result of a 90 percent bilateral trade loss.

Figure B.1
Estimated Effect on GDP of Bilateral Trade Losses Because of War

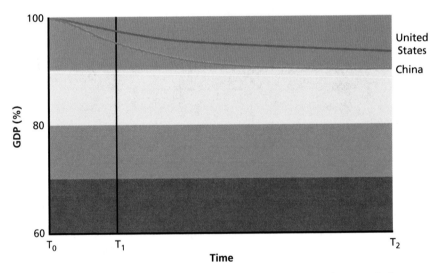

NOTES: This graph illustrates the percentage by which GDP may decrease during war as a result of bilateral trade losses. The upper limit of the y-axis indicates GDP at the start of war; as the war continues, GDP at each point in time is given as a percentage of GDP at the start of war.
RAND RR1140-B.1

Figure B.2
Estimated Effect on GDP of Overall Trade Losses Because of War

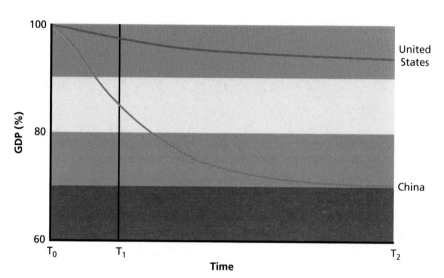

NOTES: This graph illustrates the percentage by which GDP may decrease during war as a result of overall (bilateral, regional, and global) trade losses. The upper limit of the y-axis indicates GDP at the start of war; as the war continues, GDP at each point in time is given as a percentage of GDP at the start of war.
RAND RR1140-B.2

- China would suffer a 30 percent decrease in GDP after one year as a result of a 90 percent bilateral trade loss, an 80 percent East Asian regional trade loss, and a 50 percent global trade loss (because of the postulated "war zone" effect on seaborne trade in the Western Pacific).

Consumption

- Because the trade effects described above take account of some of the consumption effects, this analysis of consumption effects presents an upper bound.

U.S. Losses

- Hess found that there is a 4 percent decline in consumption because of war away from home.[4]
- U.S. consumption in 2013 equaled 68 percent of GDP.
- The United States could suffer a 3 percent decrease in GDP after one year as a result of a decline in consumption.

China's Losses

- Hess found that there is a 4.4 percent loss in consumption because of war at home.[5]
- China's consumption in 2013 equaled 34 percent of GDP.
- China could suffer a 2 percent decrease in GDP after one year as a result of a decline in consumption.
- With a higher consumption share (60 percent of GDP), there would be a 3 percent decrease in GDP after one year because of consumption loss.

---

[4] Gregory D. Hess, "The Economic Welfare Cost of Conflict: An Empirical Assessment," Working Paper No. 852, Munich, Germany: Center for Economic Studies and Ifo Institute for Economic Research, February 2003, p. 12.

[5] Hess, 2003, p. 12.

Abbreviations

A2AD	anti-access and area denial
ASAT	anti-satellite
ASW	anti-submarine warfare
C2	command and control
C4ISR	command, control, communications, computing, intelligence, surveillance, and reconnaissance
EEZ	Exclusive Economic Zone
GDP	gross domestic product
INF	Intermediate-Range Nuclear Forces
ISIS	Islamic State of Iraq and Syria
ISR	intelligence, surveillance, and reconnaissance
MLRS	multiple launch rocket system
NATO	North Atlantic Treaty Organization
PLA	People's Liberation Army
PLAN	People's Liberation Army Navy

Bibliography

Alberts, David, and Richard E. Hayes, *Power to the Edge: Command and Control in the Information Age*, Washington, D.C.: U.S. Department of Defense Command and Control Research Program, 2003.

Balke, Nathan S., Stephen P. A. Brown, and Mine Kuban Yucel, *Oil Price Shocks and U.S. Economic Activity: An International Perspective*, Discussion Paper 10-37, Washington, D.C.: Resources for the Future, July 23, 2010.

Barro, Robert J., "Rare Disasters and Asset Markets in the Twentieth Century," *Quarterly Journal of Economics*, Vol. 121, No. 3, August 2006, pp. 823–866.

Barro, Robert J., and Charles J. Redlick, "Macroeconomic Effects from Government Purchases and Taxes," *Quarterly Journal of Economics*, Vol. 126, No. 1, 2011, pp. 51–102.

Bi, Jianxiang, "Joint Operations: Developing a New Paradigm," in James Mulvenon and David M. Finkelstein, eds., *China's Revolution in Doctrinal Affairs: Emerging Trends in the Operational Art of the Chinese People's Liberation Army*, Washington, D.C.: CNA Corporation, December 2005, pp. 29–78.

Blasko, Dennis J., "The PLA Army/Ground Forces," in Kevin Pollpeter and Kenneth Allen, eds., *The PLA as Organization v2.0*, Vienna, Va.: Defense Group Inc., 2015.

Borg, Scott, "How Cyber Attacks Will Be Used in International Conflict," paper presented at the USENIX Security Technology Symposium, Washington, D.C., 2010.

Cavaiola, Lawrence, David Gompert, and Martin Libicki, "Cyber House Rules: On War, Retaliation and Escalation," *Survival: Global Politics and Strategy*, Vol. 57, No. 1, February–March 2015.

"The Centenary Delusion," *The Economist*, January 3, 2015. As of January 22, 2015:
http://www.economist.com/news/asia/21637440-asia-2014-was-not-europe-1914-after-all-echoes-warrant-heeding-centenary-delusion

Center for Strategic and International Studies, "Long-Term Growth Rates: Can China Maintain Its Current Growth?" Washington, D.C., October 2009. As of June 5, 2015:
http://csis.org/files/publication/091019_china-bal_3-Long-Term-Growth-Rates.pdf

Chase, Michael S., Jeffrey G. Engstrom, Tai Ming Cheung, Kristen Gunness, Scott Warren Harold, Susan Puska, and Samuel K. Berkowitz, *China's Incomplete Military Transformation: Assessing the Weaknesses of the People's Liberation Army (PLA)*, Santa Monica, Calif.: RAND Corporation, RR-893-USCC, 2015. As of March 20, 2015:
http://www.rand.org/pubs/research_reports/RR893.html

"China Makes First Announcement on Strategic Oil Reserves," Reuters, November 20, 2014. As of January 22, 2015:
http://www.reuters.com/article/2014/11/20/china-oil-reserves-idUSL3N0TA1QE20141120

Congressional-Executive Commission on China, *2014 Annual Report*, Washington, D.C., October 9, 2014. As of January 22, 2015:
http://www.cecc.gov/publications/annual-reports/2014-annual-report

Davis, Bob, "China Growth Seen Slowing Sharply over Decade," *The Wall Street Journal*, October 20, 2014. As of June 5, 2015:
http://www.wsj.com/articles/china-growth-seen-slowing-sharply-over-decade-1413778141

Economy, Elizabeth C., "China's Imperial President: Xi Jinping Tightens His Grip," *Foreign Affairs*, November–December 2014, pp. 80–91.

Finkelstein, David, "Chinese Perceptions of the Costs of a Conflict," in Andrew Scobell, ed., *The Costs of Conflict: The Impact on China of a Future War*, Carlisle, Pa.: Strategic Studies Institute, U.S. Army War College, 2001, pp. 9–28.

Frankel, Jeffrey A., and David Romer, "Does Trade Cause Growth?" *American Economic Review*, Vol. 89, No. 3, June 1999, pp. 379–399.

Glick, Reuven, and Alan M. Taylor, "Collateral Damage: Trade Disruption and the Economic Impact of War," *Review of Economics and Statistics*, Vol. 92, No. 1, February 2010, pp. 102–127.

Gompert, David C., Hans Binnendijk, and Bonny Lin, *Blinders, Blunders, and Wars: What America and China Can Learn*, Santa Monica, Calif.: RAND Corporation, RR-768-RC, 2014. As of January 22, 2015:
http://www.rand.org/pubs/research_reports/RR768.html

Gompert, David C., and Terrence K. Kelly, "Escalation Cause: How the Pentagon's New Strategy Could Trigger War with China," *Foreign Policy*, August 3, 2013. As of January 22, 2015:
http://foreignpolicy.com/2013/08/03/escalation-cause

Gompert, David C., and Phillip C. Saunders, *The Paradox of Power: Sino-American Strategic Restraint in an Age of Vulnerability*, Washington, D.C.: Center for the Study of Chinese Military Affairs, National Defense University, 2011.

Greenert, Jonathan W., and Norton Schwartz, "Air-Sea Battle: Promoting Stability in an Era of Uncertainty," *The American Interest*, February 20, 2012. As of January 22, 2015:
http://www.the-american-interest.com/2012/02/20/air-sea-battle/

Henley, Lonnie, "War Control: Chinese Concepts of Escalation Management," in Andrew Scobell and Larry M. Wortzel, eds., *Shaping China's Security Environment: The Role of the People's Liberation Army*, Carlisle, Pa.: Strategic Studies Institute, U.S. Army War College, 2006, pp. 81–103.

Hess, Gregory D., "The Economic Welfare Cost of Conflict: An Empirical Assessment," Working Paper No. 852, Munich, Germany: Center for Economic Studies and Ifo Institute for Economic Research, February 2003.

Huang, Yukon, "China's Misleading Economic Indicators," *Financial Times*, August 29, 2014. As of June 5, 2015:
http://carnegieendowment.org/2014/08/29/china-s-misleading-economic-indicators

International Monetary Fund, World Economic Outlook Database, October 2014. As of January 28, 2015:
http://www.imf.org/external/pubs/ft/weo/2014/02/weodata/weoselgr.aspx

Kelly, Terrence K., David C. Gompert, and Duncan Long, *Smarter Power, Stronger Partners: Exploiting U.S. Advantages to Prevent Aggression*, Santa Monica, Calif.: RAND Corporation, RR-1359-A, forthcoming

Kowalski, Alex, "Recession Took Bigger Bite Than Estimated," *Bloomberg*, July 29, 2011. As of January 22, 2015:
http://www.bloomberg.com/news/2011-07-29/recession-took-bigger-bite-out-of-u-s-economy-than-previously-estimated.html

Lieberthal, Kenneth, and Wang Jisi, *Addressing U.S.-Chinese Strategic Distrust*, Washington, D.C.: John L. Thornton China Center, Brookings Institution, 2012.

Liu Shenyang, "On War of Control—Mainly from the Military Thinking Perspective," *China Military Science*, April 2014, pp. 1–8.

Kamiya Matake, "Japanese Public Opinions About the Exercise of the Right of Collective Self-Defense," *Discuss Japan*, September 25, 2014. As of July 20, 2015:
http://www.japanpolicyforum.jp/en/archives/politics/pt20140925231907.html

Office of the Secretary of Defense, *Annual Report to Congress: Military and Security Developments Involving the People's Republic of China 2014*, Washington, D.C., April 24, 2014. As of January 22, 2015:
http://www.defense.gov/pubs/2014_DoD_China_Report.pdf

Parker, Geoffrey, "The Military Revolution," in Lawrence Freedman, ed., *War*, Oxford, UK: Oxford University Press, Oxford, 1994, pp. 247–253.

Peng Guangqian and Yao Youzhi, eds., *Science of Military Strategy* [*Zhanlue Xue*], Beijing: Military Science Press, 2005.

Pomfret, John, "U.S. Takes a Tougher Tone with China," *The Washington Post*, July 30, 2010.

Schwartz, Norton A., and Jonathan W. Greenert, "Air-Sea Battle: Promoting Stability in an Era of Uncertainty," *The American Interest*, February 20, 2012.

Scissors, Derek, "China's Real GDP [Growth] Is Slower Than Official Figures Show," *Financial Times*, January 20, 2015. As of June 5, 2015:
http://blogs.ft.com/beyond-brics/2015/01/20/
guest-post-chinas-real-gdp-is-slower-than-official-figures-show/

Sevastianova, Daria, "Impact of War on Country per Capita GDP: A Descriptive Analysis," *Peace Economics, Peace Science, and Public Policy*, Vol. 15, No. 1, 2009, pp. 1–28.

Shanker, Thom, "Warning Against Wars Like Iraq and Afghanistan," *The New York Times*, February 25, 2011. As of July 6, 2015:
http://www.nytimes.com/2011/02/26/world/26gates.html?_r=0

Stockholm International Peace Research Institute, *SIPRI Yearbook 2014: Armaments, Disarmament and International Security*, Oxford, UK: Oxford University Press, 2014.

U.S. Bureau of Economic Analysis, "Balance of Payments and Direct Investment Position Data (U.S. Direct Investment Position Abroad on a Historical-Cost Basis and Foreign Direct Investment Position in the United States on a Historical-Cost Basis)," n.d. As of January 28, 2015:
http://www.bea.gov/iTable/index_MNC.cfm

U.S. Census Bureau, "2013: U.S. Trade in Goods with China," 2013. As of January 28, 2015:
http://www.census.gov/foreign-trade/balance/c5700.html#2013

U.S. Department of the Treasury, Federal Reserve Bank of New York, and Board of Governors of the Federal Reserve System, *Foreign Portfolio Holdings of U.S. Securities*, April 2014. As of January 28, 2015:
http://www.treasury.gov/ticdata/Publish/shla2013r.pdf

U.S. Naval Institute, "Document: Air Sea Battle Name Change Memo," January 20, 2015. As of January 22, 2015:
http://news.usni.org/2015/01/20/document-air-sea-battle-name-change-memo

Work, Robert, Deputy Secretary of Defense, statement to the Council of Foreign Relations, January 20, 2015. As of January 22, 2015:
http://www.cfr.org/defense-and-security/
deputy-secretary-defense-robert-work-asia-pacific-rebalance/p33538

World Bank, *China Economic Update: Special Topic—Changing Food Consumption Patterns in China; Implications for Domestic Supply and International Trade*, Beijing, June 2014a. As of July 20, 2015:
http://www.worldbank.org/content/dam/Worldbank/document/EAP/China/China_Economic_Update_June2014.pdf

———, "Household Final Consumption Expenditure, etc. (% of GDP)," World Development Indicators, 2014b. As of January 28, 2015:
http://data.worldbank.org/indicator/NE.CON.PETC.ZS

World Trade Organization, "China," trade profile, September 2014. As of January 28, 2015:
http://stat.wto.org/CountryProfile/WSDBCountryPFView.aspx?Language=E&Country=CN

Zhang Yuliang, ed., *Science of Campaigns* [*Zhanyi Xue*], Beijing: National Defense University Press, 2006.